Fragments

CW01023844

Jean Baudrillard is one of the most revered philosophers of the past century, and his work has helped define how we think about the postmodern. In this fascinating book of interviews conducted with François L'Yvonnet, Baudrillard is on sparkling form and explores his life in terms of his educational, political and literary experiences, as well as reflecting on his intellectual genesis and his position as outsider in the field of great French thinkers. Perhaps most interestingly, Baudrillard discusses his life's work in relation to his contemporaries: thinkers such as Bataille and the Situationists, Barthes, Lyotard and Deleuze, among others.

Instead of examining his work as a project of intellectual accumulation, Baudrillard challenges all the major interpretations of his work by suggesting he has always adopted an anti-system, anti-totality strategy – here termed an 'aphoristic strategy'. Even globalization is accompanied in his view by a Western culture which itself is no longer a well-founded confident universalism. The system of Western culture is subject today to radical uncertainty and chaos. Such fractalization can be opposed in Baudrillard's view only by the radical form of symbolic fragment, the aphorism and the singularity for 'this form alone attacks the system'.

Fragments: Conversations with François L'Yvonnet will be essential reading for any scholar of Baudrillard, but will also prove an attractive and informative starting point for any student trying to get to grips with his work for the first time.

Jean Baudrillard is author of *Cool Memories I–IV*, *The Perfect Crime*, *America* and *Simulacra and Simulation*, among other books.

Fragments
Conversations with François L'Yvonnet

Jean Baudrillard

Translated by Chris Turner
with a foreword by
Mike Gane

Routledge
Taylor & Francis Group

LONDON AND NEW YORK

First published 2001 as *D'un Fragment L'autre*
by Editions Albin Michel S.A., Paris

English translation published 2004
by Routledge
11 New Fetter Lane, London EC4P 4EE

Simultaneously published in the USA and Canada
by Routledge
29 West 35th Street, New York, NY 10001

Routledge is an imprint of the Taylor & Francis Group

© 2001 Editions Albin Michel S.A., 22 rue Huyghens,
75014 Paris
© 2004 Chris Turner for translation and footnotes, and Mike Gane
for foreword and footnotes

Typeset in Garamond by BC Typesetting Ltd, Bristol
Printed and bound in Great Britain by
TJ International Ltd, Padstow, Cornwall

British Library Cataloguing in Publication Data
A catalogue record for this book is available from the British Library

Library of Congress Cataloging in Publication Data
Baudrillard, Jean.
   [D'un fragment l'autre. English]
   Fragments/by Jean Baudrillard; translated by Chris Turner;
with a foreword by Mike Gane.
      p.   cm.
Includes bibliographical references and index.
   1. Baudrillard, Jean–Interviews. I. Turner, Chris. II. Title.
   B2430.B33974A5 2003
   194–dc22   2003009852

ISBN 0–415–30547–0 (hbk)
ISBN 0–415–30548–9 (pbk)

I had a dream about reality.
It was such a relief to wake up.
Stanislaw J. Lec*

* *Unkempt Thoughts* (New York: St. Martin's Press, 1962), p. 154.

Contents

Foreword

This book, first published in France in 2001, is a set of interviews in which François L'Yvonnet questions Jean Baudrillard about his life and writings. Although Baudrillard has talked about his intellectual biography before, much more is revealed here about direct influences and encounters with ideas and authors than ever before. And in the course of the interviews Baudrillard provides a detailed exposition of his thinking on the eve of September 11.

Born in Reims in north-eastern France in 1929, Jean Baudrillard has become one of France's most celebrated – and notorious – thinkers. After an initial formation in languages and literature, he taught German at *lycée* level for many years. He converted to sociology in the 1960s, taking up a teaching post at the University at Nanterre. In the early 1960s he was widely known as a prolific translator of Peter Weiss, Marx, Mühlmann and others from German into French. But from 1968 he began a prodigious career as a social analyst. At first his works were concerned with developing a semiotic analysis of consumer culture from a utopian Marxist viewpoint tinged, as he explains here, with a radicalism derived from 'pataphysics' and 'Situationism' which was perfectly in line with the student movement which dominated the events of 1968. From these interviews we also learn that he was involved with Félix Guattari in a Franco-Chinese association around 1964. Baudrillard followed the Cultural Revolution in China closely and supported it – for his

'far left' group even tried to get official recognition from the
Chinese government (Chapter 2); we learn that he edited the publications of the association. Soon after, he was editing the
'Situationist' style journal called *Utopie*, which examined French
culture from a position that was quite different from the orthodox
Marxism coming from the philosophers or from the French
Communist Party. Baudrillard's analysis was concerned to show
the effects of consumerism and affluence on the mode of social
integration, involving, he said, a shift from repression to enjoy-
ment and pleasure. While at the same time he remained
committed to an explicitly utopian messianic perspective his
academic publications on consumerism apply a semiotic method
in the manner of Roland Barthes, whose work he has always
insisted provided a model.

After the failure of the student rebellion of those years,
Baudrillard wrote a critique of Marxism and 'political economy'
as a theoretical system – not for being too radical, but for not
being radical enough. Marxist theory was, he said, insufficiently
critical of the very framework assumptions of political economy.
He began to define a new critique in the opposition between
symbolic exchange as represented in the gift (he drew attention
to Marcel Mauss's famous essay) on the one hand, and commodity
and object sign-exchange on the other. In effect his thematic and
methodology became anthropological rather than semiological, or
rather the former became the basis of a highly critical relation to
the latter (which became for him expressive of, and complicit
with, contemporary culture itself). His programme of writing
that followed explored themes such as fate, seduction and evil, in
which Baudrillard drew on classic anthropology, studies of messianic movements, linguistics and world literature (for example,
Taoist classics). From this radical anthropology Baudrillard
drew up a new account of the development of Western culture
through stages of simulacra from the Renaissance onwards.
These orders suggest the way in which Western culture has
constructed 'reality' as an external nature but only later to virtua-
lize it. If the first stage, the eighteenth century, produced a natural
order of simple automata, and the second, the nineteenth century,

an order of factories and robots, the third stage, the twentieth century, introduced the computer and the mass mediation of cultures of the consumer society. But Baudrillard's subsequent work suggests that the pure consumer age was relatively short and that a fourth order is now predominant in Western culture. It is in connection with this shift to the information age and radical uncertainty that he introduces the concept of the particularity, the singularity, the fragment.

It is clear from this set of interviews that Baudrillard's current thought seeks to define the fragment in a way that links it to his long-term concern with the symbolic. What makes his recent writing so enigmatic is that many of his key ideas are now expressed in a reversed form, for example symbolic exchange (for example the gift) is today discussed as 'impossible exchange'. This is because his analysis of fourth-order simulation proposes that a fundamental inversion in time–space has occurred at the heart of the information revolution. In these interviews Baudrillard explains the meaning of this thesis, and in so doing reveals how he conceives his work to have continued its search for a radical opposition to cultural totalitarianism, virtualization and globalization.

Mike Gane

Translator's note

Mike Gane and I have greatly increased the number of notes in this edition in order to make some of the topics discussed more accessible to an English readership. The additional notes are simply marked with an asterisk.

Chris Turner

1 Untimely fragments

Following Nietzsche's advice, we might sound out concepts with a hammer. This might perhaps be a good way of conducting our interviews. Nietzsche, whose searing words accompanied you through adolescence.

It was a relationship that went in fits and starts, so to speak, and there was even an enormous period of eclipse in it. I was a great devotee of Nietzsche. I read him very early, in the sixth form. I was even lucky enough to have him in both the written and oral German *agrégation* exams, though that was my undoing, as the examiners didn't agree at all with my reading; Nietzsche took his revenge there, unless we take the view that he did me a favour by preventing me from passing the exam. After that, I stopped reading him entirely. I held him in a kind of quasi-visceral memory, but I'd only retained what *I* wanted to. I would remember particular aspects of his thought, or find aspects of it emerging in a more or less aphoristic memory. There was a long eclipse, but I was already on the ecliptic. All in all, Nietzsche was never, strictly speaking, a reference for me, but an ingrained memory.

Yet there was a time when he was a required reference, from Michel Foucault to Gilles Deleuze, not to mention Jean-François Lyotard, Philippe Sollers and company. Everyone had his own little portable Nietzsche, vying in debate about him at the fashionable conferences!

The debates on Nietzsche left me quite cold. On the other hand, I'm taken now with the idea of reading him in German again. At the end of a cycle, you come back, if not to the starting point, then at least to something inaugural, which may be very intense! But I don't like to be labelled, even in relation to the finest works. I'm not saying something has changed. Nietzsche is in me in the mode of the *unzeitgemäss*, as he puts it himself, the mode of the *untimely*.

All the same, the starting point, the point at which I began to write, was a certain state of current events. I'd forgotten the searing intensity of Nietzsche and had moved more directly into the political sphere, the semio-sociological sphere.

In talking with you about Nietzsche, I was thinking in particular of the genealogical method which enables us to uncover what lies hidden behind ideas, to see their real basis.

That was the method I followed, but my material came from worldly affairs. There are no other ways of thinking, it seems to me. In this sense, Nietzsche really is a unique thinker. I don't see any other like him. But my philosophical background is shaky, particularly where the classical philosophers are concerned, such as Kant and Hegel, or even Heidegger. I've read him of course, but not in the German, and fragmentarily. Perhaps one only ever studies one philosopher seriously, just as one has only one godfather, as one has only a single idea in one's life.[1] Nietzsche is, then, the author beneath whose broad shadow I moved, though involuntarily, and without even really knowing I was doing so. I've quoted him at times, but not often. And I've never even thought of mobilizing or adapting him for my own ends. If I come back to him again now, this is doubtless because I'm going back to the aphoristic form, in writing or photography. Though Nietzschean aphorisms are often of such scope that they're perhaps something other than aphorisms. At any rate, you can use Nietzsche aphoristically, and not philosophically or ideologically.

Or politically, of course. You say that one only ever has one great thought in one's life. This runs counter to a tenacious and very modern illusion, which claims to measure a thinker's work by the permanent novelty of its themes! As though, down the ages, the great philosophies hadn't been concerned, first and foremost, to draw out all the consequences from a single, great idea.

You can have thousands of ideas, but a thought [*une pensée*] is something else! I do in fact believe you only ever have one in your life.

What is your thought, the one that was in you from the start?

This is a good, but mistaken, question. It's not possible to conceive the omega point from which you might look on that ultimately rather nebulous constellation that is a personal thought.

I'm thinking, for example, of Clément Rosset,[2] of whom it might be said that his entire work has consisted simply in asserting the simplicity of the real, its 'idiocy', and that all he has ever done is go deeper into this youthful 'intuition'. Or Descartes would be another example, and the three dreams which revealed the famous method to him. In each case, quite early thoughts!

The first obsession I remember is an obsession with the object, but understood in a somewhat magical sense. Behind the critique of objects, and of the system of objects, of the consumer society, there was the magic of the object – in this case, an ideal object. At any rate, a clear desire to sweep away the whole culture based on the philosophical subject.

We're back with Nietzsche here, mocking the subject – the 'I' that is only ever a grammatical fiction. 'For in the past one believed in the "soul", as one believed in "grammar".'[3]

Admittedly Nietzsche plays a part here, but there's another root too: pataphysics.[4] The dealings I had with pataphysics I owe first to my philosophy teacher, Emmanuel P., who was later to preside over the College of Pataphysics.

You attended the lycée *at Reims, the land of the 'Grand Jeu': René Daumal, Roger Gilbert-Lecomte, Roger Vailland and their common project 'of making men despair of themselves and society'.*[5]

P. talked about it to us, but I didn't discover the 'Grand Jeu' until later. It's a school of thought I do recognize, and with which I feel a certain affinity, and I even admit that the fact an intellectual adventure of that nature took place in my native city, Reims — for which I'm not, however, particularly nostalgic — gives me a certain pleasure. To come back to pataphysics, for me, particularly at the beginning, it was a kind of rather fierce clearing of the decks.

What was so fiercely cleared away?

I was a very good pupil at the *lycée*. In particular, I had an amazing memory. And, at a certain moment, I came to repent of all that, I had my youthful Rimbaud moment. Making the *sacrificio del intelletto* — that was the impact of pataphysics on my existence. This would perhaps have happened in other ways, but it has to be admitted that the pataphysical acid, the pataphysical detergent was very virulent. From the outset with me, there was a kind of very powerful cultural counter-transference.

The idea of starting out from scratch, of sweeping away all I'd accumulated. During my secondary school years, I'd achieved quite a sizeable primitive accumulation — and indeed it served me cynically at University where, without doing any work at all, I was able to pass my exams easily. So the break came there! My first writings weren't essays, but texts difficult to classify, poetic texts, if I may use that term, which were brought together in my book, *L'Ange de stuc*. There were others before, but I burned them. My first relationship to language was much more visceral or poetic than conceptual.

And in a way you're coming back to that.

You could certainly say I've come to a point where I want, for example, to take up again the translation I made of Hölderlin, and to take up Nietzsche again too, and even pataphysics, which re-emerges in a certain context of analysis, at the end of a theorization of integral reality, of the realization of the world through all our techniques and systems. Once achieved, this integral reality is the Ubuesque accomplishment *par excellence*! Pataphysics might be said to be the only response to this phenomenon, both in its total confusion – it's neither critical nor transcendent, it's the perfect tautology of this integral reality, it's the science of sciences – and at the same time it's the monstrousness of it too. Pataphysics is both a science of imaginary solutions and a myth of imaginary solutions. It's the imaginary solution to the kind of final solution that the current state of affairs might be said to constitute.

If there is a return to pataphysics, it's not in terms of argument or solutions, but a return that is itself imaginary, a kind of singular horizon. But I don't have any inclination to argue about this; it would be entirely paradoxical, since there's no reason to lend any philosophical or metaphysical status to the adventure! Pataphysics remains a game, and at the same time a violent ferment. I had the opportunity to say what I thought about it in a piece I wrote on Artaud and pataphysics in a poetico-metaphorical style. I was about twenty at the time and I was torn between the two. I contrasted the theatre of cruelty, of bloody, savage, raw cruelty, with pataphysics, which is exactly the opposite. For pataphysics there is no primal scene. There is nothing in a raw, cruel state. Everything is already a virtual phantasmagoria. This text was directly addressed to Emmanuel P., whose story Henri Thomas has written in his novel, *La Saison volée*, an allusion to Rimbaud's book, of which P. had a first edition.[6]

Ultimately, for me, pataphysics was a kind of esoteric paren-
thesis. But, in the end, considering this integral reality, this
kind of integrism of reality – of the real and the rational – we
find ourselves unwittingly in an entirely pataphysical situation!

Ubuesque in spite of itself!

But we must avoid any conflation here, and preserve the fantastical
aura of pataphysics, keep it as a radical external hypothesis.
It remains precious for describing this full, overfull world,
saturated like King Ubu, who's the image of overblown, self-
satisfied cruelty – which corresponds rather well to our current
environment!

When he's bored, Ubu decides to make war!

And shuts up his conscience in his suitcase.[7] But pataphysics isn't
a reference for me either. Things have to be lost! Whether we're
talking of Nietzsche, Hölderlin, pataphysics or anything else,
these thoughts have to be anagrammatized in what one does.
That is to say, the concept or definition has to pass out of sight;
they have to be there only in the anagrammatic state. All this
has to disappear, to scatter, like the anagram of the name of
God in the poem.

*One thinks of Borges and his fine pages on the Kabbalah, which, he says,
is not a museum object but a metaphor for thought.*[8]

Borges, who was a member of my imaginary list of authors, my
ideal bestiary – if you want to indulge in this kind of mental
game – alongside Walter Benjamin and Roland Barthes. Only
Bs, as it happens, as Baudelaire's also in there.

A lineage is always constructed a posteriori, *to converge on the person
laying claim to it. It doesn't exist in itself, but only through its destination! You have to be capable of taking it over without the aid of teleology.*

It is, admittedly, always a kind of ideal retrospective. We should add Rimbaud or Artaud. It was that poetic vein I initially felt was mine.

Is the notion of cruelty – the pursuit of destructive contradictions by systematic recourse to dissonance – in the way that Antonin Artaud developed its themes so profusely, still operative?

Artaud dreams of eliminating representation, which gets in the way of the body, the body in its cruelty. The body is there, even if it isn't easy to live it; it is the actor in its own dramaturgy. The point, for him, was to find a theatre that could convey that, but I don't think any theatre, beginning with his own, really matches up to his ideals. You don't achieve that by piling on violence and incest! Can one still think in terms of cruelty, of blood as opposed to meaning? Is such a flaying of the skin still possible? There's no one who can be easily compared with Artaud in his singularity. And there's no point merely extending or repeating what he did, even if it corresponds to the barrenness of a certain universe.

There remains all the same a desire for a generalized subversion of the underpinnings of metaphysics.

For Artaud, there's still a body, the convolutions of the body, including sex, which is a sort of total harassment. There's the desire to eliminate all that to get down to some sort of matter or other. There's the dream of a base level, of an atrocity, a ferocity, a savagery we've all dreamed of to some extent. But today we can dream of a radical alternative, that of evil, which lies not in a violence that comes from the body, but in a more metaphysical violence – the violence of illusion, for example. In a way, Artaud was also in illusion. Cruelty is, indeed, an illusion, and the world is cruel because it's illusion. But I find it hard to connect this experience of cruelty with today's world.

Artaud and Pataphysics – and I was equally attached to both – seem irreconcilable. The pataphysical world is much more

despairing than that of Artaud, who catches the imagination, who
has a language. A language that is perhaps the language of madness, a glossolalia, but, all the same, the cruelty is spoken and that
counts for something. There's ultimately the possibility, if not of
representation, then at least of a symbolic dramaturgy. You find
this also with the Spanish photographer Nebreda, who plays on
his body, his death, but who always, ultimately, has it available
to him to speak this, to produce it as eructation. There is an –
in this case, non-linguistic – act, an 'acting-out', at the confines
of an impossible situation. Nebreda has locked himself away for
twenty years, but he's photographed himself with consummate
art, with total virtuosity.

Artaud also provides an opportunity to ask an essential question: what can be done with irreducible singularities? Everything
we're saying here is meaningful discourse. With those who are
both acted by, and actors of, that discourse, you can't, in a sense,
do anything; you can't draw lessons from them, nor analyse the
rest of the world through their experience. Each person should
have an unyielding singularity, but not everyone has the good
fortune to be mad or, like Andy Warhol, to be a machine.

Is there still room for singularities?

We can hope so. The only ones you see emerging – whether
political singularities or other kinds – are largely reactional or
abreactional. Where art is concerned, it's hard to see what
would be an alternative. You have the impression that all the production is part of the same world. For pataphysics there's no
longer any singularity. The *grande Gidouille* is no longer a singularity, it is a transcendent ventriloquism, to use Lichtenberg's
expression. We're all *Palotins*[9] in a gaseous world from which the
great pataphysical fart is released. Artaud is the extremity, the
extreme limit of a metaphysics turned cruel, but there's still
the glimmer of a metaphysical hope, there's a savage recrimination
that's metaphysical in nature, whereas Pataphysics, as its name
suggests, has swept all that away. We're not going to make it

into an ultimate authority either; if it is a culmination, it's only in the sense that it's an abolition. There's no illusion in it, but pure illusionism, full stop. As hypercritical or ultra-critical thought – much more critical than critical thought – there's nothing better.

There is perhaps still a possibility of breaking through.

Perhaps recovering an illusion, both radical and cruel, that might reflect the world as it is. The illusion of the world exists if you know how to see it. It isn't necessarily violent, it's something else; it's a parallel universe. Life itself is a parallel universe: 'Life is what happens to us while we're doing something else.' In a totalized, centred, concentric universe, only eccentric possibilities are left. Everywhere parallel processes, parallel societies, parallel markets are establishing themselves. Integration necessarily produces eccentric zones, for better or for worse.

In singularity you also find excess.

Indeed, you do. This is another aspect of what I've called the 'showing-through' [*transparition*] of evil. The world, as it is in its cruelty, is evil. If you try to stem that evil, to reduce it, meta-stases and excrescences will be produced, such as the ones we're speaking of. That's what interests me most right now – parallel universes. Even if I'm not capable of following all the developments in particle physics, there are some very interesting things being said there about parallel universes. But there's no need to look in physics; it's all here!

If you haven't read the great philosophers, or haven't read them much, you've at least made hay with literature, and not just French literature, even if it was in a 'free' way.

That's true. Lots of novels, such as those of Faulkner, Dostoyevsky, Stendhal and, later, lots of American novelists.

And Céline?

Yes, but he's an exception. His work is so explosive and inimitable. All those who've tried to throw themselves into it have come to grief. From the moment I went into theory, into analysis, so to speak, the other lineage came into play, that of Nietzsche and Hölderlin! All this is very difficult to reconstitute. More recently, I've read more novels – Vladimir Nabokov, Saul Bellow, Guido Ceronetti. The reference here is no longer to the history of ideas. What more can I say? To go deeply into this you'd have to make the effort to retrace your own footprints. But since I've done all I can to obliterate them, it becomes difficult even for me to exhume them. At any rate, it hasn't been an evolutionary development; I don't believe that's ever the case with culture in general. Each moment has an incomparable singularity. There's no accumulation and hence not really any evolution – no overall goal. With this obsession, into the bargain, that's almost a perversion, of trying to forget, to obliterate, to eliminate things – the things closest to me.

For example, I felt a great affinity with Roland Barthes precisely to the extent that he evinced a desire to surround what he said with an extraordinary protection, so that you could approach it only in a kind of reflectiveness, a kind of contemplation – and not at all an affiliation. Feeling so close, I assumed a defensive distance. At any rate, one thing's certain: you can't put these different influences into any continuous, cumulative history.

Above all, don't try to situate yourself in a coherent, vectorized history of ideas, with determining influences, paternities, impeccable filiations.

Above all, don't do that. I even have a bias against that kind of misguided preoccupation with references.

Every thought is based on other thoughts. How can one do otherwise? But in your writing the system of references operates in a quite peculiar way, at least not in an academic way. One has only to read your books; footnotes –

which normally attest to the serious nature of scholarly publications – are virtually absent!

It's true, there aren't many. I've chosen to forget them! Which gives translators a lot of trouble. This isn't affectation on my part! Even if something comes to me from afar, it has to be as though I invented it myself.

I believe it was Oscar Wilde who said a man with a little education always quotes imperfectly.

I have even used completely imaginary quotations.

A very Borges-like thing to do!

The funniest being the one that stands as an epigraph to a chapter in *Simulacre et Simulation*, falsely attributed to Ecclesiastes: 'The simulacrum is never that which conceals the truth – it is truth which conceals that there is none. The simulacrum is true.' Nobody spotted it! Except for a Swiss reader who, having greatly liked the quotation, went looking for it in the Bible – and didn't, of course, find it! She wrote in despair, asking me to help her out!

People are convinced the Bible is inexhaustible and that you can find everything in it! Everything and its opposite.

That's true in a way! But in the case in question the concepts weren't very biblical! My bias in these matters is preferential, so to speak, not referential. I reject the scenarios of academic research. I've never really considered the – ultimately, rather complex – question of the status of references, as those who use them – sometimes very brilliantly – must have. Jacques Derrida, for example, must surely have some idea of what the use of reference represents, of what the fact of always writing books about other books may mean. It's even probable, but to take this into account, to use it – or even abuse it – is alien to me.

In the case of Derrida, there's the whole tradition of Jewish and phenom-
enological hermeneutics. He argues that writing – the archi-écriture
which encompasses the whole of language – is primary in relation to
speech [la parole]*! So the written reference is originary!*

Doubtless it's impossible to do without references. But they have
to return to secrecy. The centre of gravity lies in what we do; that
must be the well-spring, and that's all there is to it. And we may
also possibly – why not? – reinvent quite simple things we may
have found elsewhere.

I have in mind something that was quite subversive among the Situation-
ists. Their call to plagiarize and be plagiarized, a rejection of all appro-
priation, even intellectual appropriation! Every thought, as soon as it is
public, belongs legitimately to the person who makes use of it.

There's no basis in this area for any property rights. At a pinch,
you might even adopt the cynical point of view that something
that can be stolen from you doesn't truly belong to you as your
own. It's for each person to have their own ideas, but above all
to have a form, for ideas can be plundered, their content can be
siphoned off anywhere! Form is something else. It's up to everyone
to have an original form.

Style, in the way Gilles-Gaston Granger speaks of it, which isn't merely
a modality of expression, but a tone of thinking. Or, again, as
Gombrowicz suggests, a mental posture consisting of brief, unthematized
illuminations.

It's incomparable and inimitable and even, in a way, inalienable.
So far as all the rest is concerned, let things circulate! I have on
occasion taken ideas from different places, when they matched
what I was thinking exactly and were better expressed than I
could have managed. As it's also happened that I've had my
ideas borrowed wholesale, without the slightest reaction of self-
defence, though I'm not going to go into that here. Admittedly,
there may be cases of deception, although this question of decep-

tion might be said to deserve closer study itself. Taken from a standpoint of truth – a discourse of truth – then all that's borrowed, plundered, etc., is questionable, reprehensible and is of the order of deception; if we aren't in that kind of discourse, things are different. There may be paradoxical, ironic uses of other people's material, as of worldly material, without offending against any great principles. I've never greatly differentiated between situations, events and texts.

It's also true that one barely recognizes oneself when other people quote what one writes!

There lies, perhaps, the real deception of quotation. I've noticed that critics often choose the quotations which show authors in a bad light, those which are the most banal expression of their discourse, and then go on to recycle that discourse to their own advantage. It's a good journalistic strategy. Quotation is never innocent. It can be a weapon, as indeed can reference, if it functions as a quotation, because there is no original referent. At bottom, it's all a matter of strategy. Being more of a *moraliste* myself, I prefer to set the meter to zero and say that what I do, I'll do alone. There is perhaps a temperamental dimension to this! What I can do, I'll do to the best of my ability, but alone. Perhaps this is a fantasy or complex of the solitary child.

In any event, the idea of operating alone is something I'm attached to. Though aware of what one is doing in this, which doesn't mean withdrawing from the world, but not exposing oneself to all kinds of vague influences, or to the random forms of current life. Exposing oneself to great authorities, yes, and to the authoritative, but without direct influence. This more mysterious, more elusive, more enigmatic path is the one I've followed.

The problem is that, in spite of yourself, a self-referential complex is created. As you write, a kind of personal heritage inevitably forms, a self-management, a personal career-path. The alternative would be to follow an aphoristic strategy in the strict sense of the word, which means to separate, to isolate from the rest, to except – to be the exceptional case each time.

2 'Activist' fragments

You actually seem to be quite a solitary person. Though you've been part of various intellectual movements and close to some groups, you've never had any affiliations to any of them, even the Situationist International.

I referred to the Situationists, but never in my writings or analyses. I spoke about them, in my lectures at Nanterre, for example. How could you not speak about them? And then, we were very close, but I never had any direct personal relations with their leaders. I knew Raoul Vaneigem a little, but I never met Guy Debord.

A solitude which brought you some unkind remarks from the S.I. In the group's journal you even came in for attack, alongside Henri Lefebvre, in articles full of name-calling. Doubtless you were paying a price for your marginality. It has to be said the Situationists had a rather curious way of referring to people.

Their attacks were aimed mainly at Henri Lefebvre, and there were undoubtedly some real issues between them. After the Father, they took against the false sons, one of whom was me. They stigmatized me as the house Maoist, all because Félix Guattari and I and a few others had set up what I think was called the Franco-Chinese People's Association, with a newspaper.

When was this?

At the time of the Cultural Revolution, in the early sixties. Félix had connections with a very committed bookshop based near the Paris Mosque, and we became quite close friends. It was his idea to found this association. We published a newspaper, the title of which I forget.[1] It ran to only two or three issues, no more than that, because the Chinese never recognized us. One of us even went to Algiers to meet Chou En-lai, but he didn't want anything to do with us. The Chinese preferred upstanding, law-abiding right-wing associations, not an uncontrollable little far-Left group! Others went to Geneva, also to meet officials from the People's Republic, but they had no more success. We organized a big meeting at the Salle des Horticulteurs that ended in violence, with OAS heavies moving in to break it up using strong-arm tactics.[2] Having no ideological baggage and not belonging to any political organization, I was just the right man to edit a paper like that! I was a bit of a front-man. The venture didn't go any further and the paper disappeared. I have happy memories of it, though it was more or less historically stillborn. It's a great story from the wild years!

Was that your last episode as an activist?

Activist is going a bit far. I've never been any kind of activist.

In Henri Lefebvre, it wasn't so much the one-time Communist that interested you, the witness to the ideological conflicts of the past, as the theorist of everyday life.

It was, certainly, the critique of everyday life that interested me. I never really took my lead from Lefebvre's work. I found what he did quite free-spirited, light and wittily written, but it seemed to me already to belong to another age, an age still closed to psychoanalysis and semiology. He wouldn't have anything to do with any of that. Structuralism was his number one enemy. And what I was doing didn't quite fit in with his own work, but we remained very good friends. When I arrived at Nanterre University in 1966–7, Lefebvre had just broken with the Situationists at the famous Strasbourg Congress.

Let's recall what that was about: in 1965, Debord broke with Lefebvre, whom he regarded as too abstract and philosophical, arguing that his book La Proclamation de la Commune *(1965) had plagiarized a Situationist pamphlet.*[3]

There were points on which we were ideologically in disagreement with the Situationists. For example, 'workers' councils' and the councils movement as a whole seemed very dated to us. On the other hand, their radicalism interested me, and everyone went along with their idea of radical subjectivity! In the end, all these things remained in the imaginary register, the political imagination. It was a phenomenon which quite rightly disappeared. That was all it could do. And those who criticize the Situationists for not having succeeded are barking up the wrong tree, since Situationism wasn't made to succeed! Today, they're reviving its ghost again, with Debord.

In Situationism, there's both an innovative, ludic thinking and, at the same time, an incredibly classical rhetoric, with ponderous theoretical demonstrations of papal seriousness, equipped with a conceptual apparatus taken directly from German philosophy – demonstrations which fascinated them. They were still in dissertation mode. Your own way of thinking and writing breaks unequivocally with all that.

They had a great force of conviction and the desire to be clear. This was the last form in which an avant-garde phenomenon of this kind appeared, though the term 'avant-garde' isn't appropriate – at any rate, a movement with such a 'pointed' critique. It was the end of a kind of revolutionary idealism, which had moved on to new ground such as daily life, the city, etc. Thanks to them, all the Marxist superstructures were greatly weakened, even if they did remain attached to old ways of thinking. All that blew away after 1970 with all the business about desire and revolution and the mixing of the two . . .

Freudo-Marxism . . .

Some saw an extreme radicalism in that. But the mix sounded the death-knell of both desire and revolution. The blending of the two led to each being neutralized by the other. There were many who based themselves on the idea for a long time. As far as the question of desire was concerned, I already had some marked disagreements with Jean-François Lyotard, and even with Gilles Deleuze . . . while entirely admiring their 'machine', which was very desirable, but from my point of view not really operative! A whole generation based themselves on this terrible ambiguity, on things that had, to all intents and purposes, already disappeared.

What makes desire and revolution irreconcilable?

The political and libidinal dimensions lose their singularity. It was their singularity alone that gave them their force. To mix the two was to contravene their irreducibility. It was, when all's said and done, one hell of a misappropriation of Marx and Freud.

Which led to neutralizing the subversive dimensions of each man's thought.

There was a kind of outpouring of the one into the other, with a total loss of intensity, to use the terms then in vogue. It would be stupid to make a pejorative analysis of this retrospectively. At the time everyone dived in, including the best minds, but, with some distance, we have to agree it was a trap, and a trap that still operates more or less everywhere today. Like the revolt of the Situationists, these ideas serve as a reference today for what I won't call the most impoverished thinking, but at least the most conventional.

We need only think of those who claim to be the heirs apparent to the Situationists today – real embezzlers of the heritage!

Let's not talk about them.

And poor old Debord, who will soon be included in the school textbooks! Isn't it always a bit suspicious for an author to become a classic so easily?

You can admire Debord's language, but that's to make an aesthetic object out of it, which wasn't the case. Form is always important, but his language wasn't an object of admiration in itself. The same thing happened when they began to analyse the thought of Freud and Marx from the ideological, emotional or even the everyday standpoint, talking about their maids and I don't know what else. To sexualize Marx and politicize Freud was a thoroughly dubious mix. This kind of mishmash or patchwork has become the vulgate today. Among the sensible critiques of Debord, one of the most pertinent came from Régis Debray. In an article which appeared, I think, in *Le Débat*, while also settling some old personal scores, he said some very apposite things about alienation, man's separation from himself. He pointed out that we weren't in that ball-game at all now; on the contrary, we're threatened not by separation or alienation, but by total immersion.

The language of the Situationists bears the hallmarks of German idealism: with the notions of alienation, objectification, reification.

I remember Situationism as something really admirable, but it's an extinct phenomenon, a dead star. Which isn't the case with Nietzsche or some others. The Situationists were like meteors, and I wouldn't want publicly to dissociate myself from them, since, in terms of events, it was an important moment. It's in the moment when things appear that their essentials are revealed.

It's in their nascent state that we should attempt to grasp movements of thought. When they have matured, they often cease to be fertile and stiffen for a last dogmatic burst before their inevitable decline.

In 1966–7, with the journal *Utopie*, we created our own little domain.[4] We developed some major objections to Situationist thinking. We were further beyond politics and ideology than they were – beyond alienation.

Utopie *also broke with the 'Bolshevik' arrogance of the Situationists, their anathemas, their improvised tribunals, their condemnations of all kinds, which ended up occupying most of their mental and militant energies. With a clear 'schoolboy' dimension evident in their wordplay.*

You're right. There was something adolescent in that revolt. For me, *Utopie* was the preparatory phase for my work on objects, on the consumer society and political economy. *The Mirror of Production* was the break with Marx, with the emergence of symbolic exchange in prospect. It was that thinking that went into *Utopie*. We were already in the transpolitical.[5]

3   Aphoristic fragments

The fragment has its ideal: a high condensation. Not of thought, or of wisdom, or of truth (as in the maxim), but of music: 'development' would be countered by 'tone,' something articulated and sung, a diction: here it is timbre which should reign.

Roland Barthes[1]

Your writing has evolved towards aphorism. For their part, the Situationists never got beyond the bon mot. *There's a world of difference between the* bon mot, *which can become a slogan to fall in behind, and the aphorism, which encourages thought.*

They were very fond of the dialectical inversion of terms. Guy Debord's *Society of the Spectacle* or Raoul Vaneigem's *Revolution of Everyday Life* are systems that unfold with an implacable logic. The Situationists didn't practice intellectual drifting, though they were the champions of urban drift,[2] of the creation of situations, but they didn't create so many of them intellectually. They set themselves up, rather, as incontestable authorities. But that's also what we liked about them, and we're not going to criticize them for it today. There was the idea – though they did it in a haughty, exclusive way – of starting out from the simplest objects, from basic situations, basic banalities,[3] and finding in them the explosive energy to reach back to the heights. And it's in the absolute detail of things that you ought to be able to find the energy to smash the totality [*ensemble*], to put an end to all totalities. And so to rediscover the world in the fragmentary state. They did this, though they didn't much do it in their theoretical writings, which are the opposite of fragments.

We're talking about the German-style treatise – Wissenschaft – *a massive, systematic thinking.*

This is what has always put me off the great German systems a little, those systems which still in a way shaped what the Situationists did. You can't read Nietzsche, Hölderlin and Sade in a continuous, constructive way. The one demolishes the other! The deconstructive work has been done, you have to come to terms with it. Now, it seems to me we still have some degree of allegiance to these great systems, Heidegger being the latest systematic totality to reign over philosophy.

You can see the difference there is, for example, between *Symbolic Exchange and Death* and the *Cool Memories* books, between, on the one hand, a book that presents things in a mode that's still theoretical, and, on the other, aphoristic writing. In the aphorism, the fragment, there is the desire to slim things down as much as possible. At that point, you no longer grasp the same things; objects are transformed when you see them in detail, in a kind of elliptical void. And this is what Lichtenberg says in one of his aphorisms. To someone who remarked that he'd put on a lot of weight, he said: 'Fat is neither soul nor body, neither flesh nor spirit; it is what the tired body produces.' We can say the same for thought: fat thought is what the tired mind produces; just like the tired body, it continues to produce, it doesn't stop, but it produces fat!

A new version of acedy.[4] *It was Leonardo da Vinci, I think, who liked to distinguish between the method of the painter, which consists in adding matter, and that of the sculptor, which consists in removing it. A work which develops, on the one hand, by accumulation and, on the other, by refinement and subtraction. You could apply this to writing – between those who build systems by adding successive elements and those who do the opposite and pare down to the fragmentary.*

It's a fine image. They are, in reality, two different forms of writing, the one which gathers things together and builds up totalized bodies of ideas and the other which, by contrast, scatters things, attentive to the details. There's the same work on detail and on the fragmentary in writing aphoristically or doing photography.

Aphoristic writing has no true legitimacy. It's recognized in France because it has a literary history to it, but it isn't in America! When the Americans read *America*, they reacted very badly.[5] Writing of that kind seemed to them the work of the devil, being a sacrilege against the canonical form of the well-argued essay. They are, in fact, right in this, and that's the whole point of it. The aphorism is, in general, quite poorly accepted. It tends, in a way, toward evil, being a violence done to discourse, but not to language.

It's true that American contemporary literature is remarkable by the size of its products. The trend is toward a thousand pages at the very least! This hypertrophy is affecting the whole of theoretical production. In France too, the most insignificant essays now to run to very great length. The more colourless the age, the more inflated the forms of expression! A curious compensatory phenomenon!

It's like organisms that grow fat to protect themselves. There is, indeed, a rash of outsized theses and scholarly works! It's like a desperate attempt to fill a void, whereas it should be the aim to find the interstice in the void. The void is the void, the point is to turn it into an – almost dramaturgical – mode of disappearance that is also a mode of thought. Though without clinging to some kind of exotic aestheticism either! It has at times been said that what I do isn't without its similarities with Oriental thought, with Chuang-Tzu, etc.

The famous butcher who slices through the gaps and openings, a parable also found in Plato in the Phaedrus *(265 e), the fine dialectician who avoids the ways of the bad carver.*[6]

But, of course, we shouldn't make Chuang-Tzu a reference either, in this case an Orientalist one. It's like Zen. You have to avoid transpositions, avoid getting into import–export. You can find inspiration or parallel, paradoxical paths, but when a form of thinking has become the dominant symbolic form, even in the East, you have to be wary of it. No thought is universal. There are only ever exceptions.

It's also the case that, in attaching the Zen epithet to you, there's perhaps, too, the secret hope you'll shut up. The sage has fallen completely silent!

Recently, when I was talking about photography and its silence, and the things I said about the worthlessness of art, there was some surprise that I could still speak about silence, as though, to be logical, I ought to keep quiet. There's no answer to that! To come back to Eastern thought – into which anything whatever is dumped – this has become a catch-all category that's as suspect as the others. I know Japan a little – China not at all – and Japanese is a language with a lot to teach us: for example, there's no word for communication, no word for the universal, no word for the subject. It's quite remarkable! But in America I found, in a sense, the same paring-down, though that wasn't in any way a Zen thing! Rather the opposite, but with the same distance from our centre of gravity. That was the America which interested me, not an objective America. If we take this other universe *en situation* – even though we have more or less the same history and share the same culture to some extent – if you take America in the raw state, then it appears like an entirely peculiar object, which carries you far from your roots. But you can't keep perpetually going over that.

These revisitings are very fashionable in publishing – not always with the same title, but with a long preface added, often self-justificatory in tone.

Along the lines of 'I was right to be right' or 'right to be wrong', or at any rate 'what I wrote was true'.

What's done is done. If it had some kind of truth, it was at a particular moment. There can be no second chance for it, no recycling. If it's lost, then so be it. If you have a modicum of self-respect, you don't go chasing after your shadow.

It's the principle of putting a message in a bottle and letting it end up where it will, unpredictably.

Perhaps one day it will be lucky enough to have its fifteen minutes of fame, as Andy Warhol put it. The aphorism consists in throwing out scattered thoughts. Every reader will variously make of them what they can. With the *Cool Memories* books, I've been able to observe that everyone takes something different from them, and that's very pleasing. You tell yourself every detail of the world can be perfect if it finds its echo. As for fame, we have to accept the idea that there must be a limited potential. The available quantity of fame[7] is not infinite. So, it's fine for everyone to have their fifteen minutes! If, by good fortune, you get a full hour, you're stealing forty-five minutes from people who won't have any. It's a bit like the theory of souls you find in some primitive cultures: there's a limited contingent of souls and there won't be any more; they do, admittedly, travel, but there are bodies waiting for souls that will never get one because the numbers are limited. It isn't a very democratic theory, but it seems more rigorous and lucid to me: the share-out of destinies.

*

It's been suggested that Pascal's Pensées *employ a rhetoric of short forms that might be said to match the fleeting nature of the human creature, who's incapable by essence of real duration and so unable to keep up sustained attention throughout a systematic treatise. Can't the same thing be said about you? Isn't the adoption of the short form a response to the times? With the video-clip or the TV advert, the fragmentary, the mobile and the instantaneous are to the fore. The aphorism might then be said to be a kind of paradoxical resistance to the dictatorship of the instant.*

The aphorism, the video-clip and the advert seem to share an instantaneity, rapidity and ephemerality, but the aphorism is different. Etymologically, *aphorizein* contains the idea of separating, isolating. It's a fragment, but a fragment that creates a whole symbolic space around it, a gap, a blank. Whereas our techniques and technologies create the instantaneous, but linked by continuity with the whole network. They are networked fragments, if I can put it that way! It's no longer possible today to establish some form of continuity, wholeness or totalization, because it will be immediately obliterated by the system itself. You have to set against it something that apparently plays by the same rules, but stands opposed to it formally. It's in the form, then – not abstractly but in a very real way. The form alone attacks the system in its very logic. Our imaginary is evolutionistic, finalistic; everything is taken for a phase or a moment in a process of becoming. If each phase or moment is taken as successive, linked, continuous, always straining towards an ideal end-goal, then all the phases are subordinated to the final phase . . .

A teleological process . . .

A well-directed, neatly programmed evolutionism! We have to break all that down by saying that at each moment each phase is perfect in its incomparable singularity, the fruit is perfect, but no more perfect than the flower.

It's the Hegelian dialectic you're talking about here: the flower which accomplishes and realizes itself in the fruit, which is the truth of the flower. You reject the whole work of the negative.

The flower is perfect. It isn't necessary to refer it to any dialectics of nature! It's the same with everything. In its detail, the world is perfect. This is what I say about photography: taken overall, at the level of meaning, the world is pretty disappointing, but each detail of the world, taken in its singularity, is perfect. You don't have to try to perfect it, because it's perfect already. It isn't about falling into pure contemplation, of course. Against wholes [*les ensembles*], against the integrist imagination, we have to move over, strategically, to the fragment, restoring its singularity to it. It's the only space you can move around in, for if a singularity is perfect in itself, you can also move from the one to the other, or play the one off against the other – there's a whole set of rules. This is reflected in all areas – in the apprehension of things, in ideas, but also in language, which is perhaps the most precious platform in this regard. Language is one of the things which resists this goal-oriented arrangement best. We have to get back to the anagrammatic use of language; if there is an idea, it has to be anagrammatized in language and so disappear as idea. There is, then, a kind of complicity here between anamorphosis, anagrams and the aphorism.

We seem close to something of the order of the fractal or fractalization.

You have to differentiate between the fractal and the fragment. The fractal presupposes a whole, which may not have existed, but it's something like the decomposition or pulverization of a whole.

With a replica of the whole in each fractal.

You're closer, then, to the hologram than to anamorphosis or the anagram. The whole is reconstituted in the detail. That is quite a productive perspective, but it seems different to me. Everything is going in that direction today: DNA, the genetic code in every cell, replication . . .

I remember an article of yours in issue no. 4 of the journal Utopie *(October 1971). It was entitled 'DNA or the metaphysics of the code' and was on Jacques Monod and his book* Chance *and* Necessity.[8]

It began like this: 'With Monod, the metaphysical principle of identity is transferred from God and the Subject to the Code and the genetic programme.'

I remember that article. I was just back from California and the Salk Institute, which was the epicentre of DNA research. There's a model for the interpretation of things in this DNA: the model of virtuality. You have a cell, a code, from which you can generate all possibilities or potentialities. What comes out of that is a cloned world! In this sense, it's the opposite of the fragment, in what is sometimes a similar guise.

In the fragment, there's the residual element – what still remains of what has been lost: we speak of the fragments of Heraclitus and, in that case, it's about a partial memory, the fragment because we don't have the whole. What you're doing is something else. With you, the fragment is a deliberate practice, the fragmentary is a rejection of totalization.

I've been through totalities [*les ensembles*] myself and, in this sense, the fragment is a product of this passage through totalities. It isn't a formal, aesthetic option. The fragmentary is the product of a resolve to destroy a totality and the will to confront emptiness and disappearance.

There's always the risk of the aphorism becoming a maxim and taking on the form of a gnomic-sounding commandment. Maxim-based thinking can be interesting, in fact, such as that of the Greeks or like the apophthegms of the Desert Fathers.

That's true. In that case, you have a directive thinking, if not indeed a moralizing thinking, with an aim of conveying meaning. It's quite difficult to distinguish between the maxim, the apophthegm and the aphorism. There's also a parallel to be drawn with photography: the image as the pre-eminent site of the fragment, of a world without goal-orientation. The image can become the site of a morality, an ideology once again, but the photograph – more than the moving image in the cinema –

seems to me to have the same privilege as the fragment, not only by the fact of selection, but also by its silence and stillness, and the fact that it, like the fragment, is linked to a suspense – something which isn't elucidated and isn't there to be elucidated.

The Heraclitean fragment is enigmatic, which earned its author the nickname 'the Obscure'.

The enigmatic aspect is at least as essential as the brevity of form. It has to remain in suspense, no meaning must carry it away. One can doubtless imagine, think or interpret, but in principle the fragment defies interpretation, or the interpretations are multiple and inexhaustible.

It's not a religious verse!

Of the kind that works only if you repeat it endlessly? Not at all. Let's take Lichtenberg, for example. You don't read his fragments to set you off on philosophical or moral digressions, or because that would fire the imagination. It's not like that at all. The fragment is meant to be decoded in its literalness. It's simply there as an object, not as a subjective formulation; like any object, it's indecipherable; it remains inexhaustible for thought.

Like the famous rose of Angelus Silesius 'which is without Why. It blooms because it blooms. It has no care of itself nor asks whether it is seen.'[9]

You have to get to that point. With Lichtenberg, it's remarkable, as his language is dense, and when you've managed to read him properly, the work is over, the reading is exhausted in the literalness of the text. It's very Barthesian too in a way. It's quite different from 'preliminary reading' [*la lecture préalable*], with the real work coming afterwards, the text being merely a pretext! You have to get to the text itself, the factuality of the language, which is not an imaginary. The concept of literalness seems very important to me, and not only for fragments. A dream – Canetti points this out – isn't meant to be deciphered, but it too must be taken literally. Leopardi, I think, says myths must be taken as they are spoken, as they form and transform in the language itself, and we must not exhaust them by interpretation, which short-circuits their power. Their power lies in the form much more than in the decipherment of a sense. Literalness is the secret of a poem, but this goes also for all forms, for any phenomenon, beginning with events, even though it is always difficult to get back to their literalness.

Which ultimately represents a major objection to any philosophy of history, which is always more or less imbued with teleology.

You have to take things in their singularity, and at the same time in their literalness. What I wrote about the metaphysics of the code in Monod, I could have written about François Furet and his metaphysics of the French Revolution.[10] To divide the French Revolution into good and bad revolutions, and then on that basis ask what went wrong, is not to know how to take an event in its literalness, with the ever-possible exponential dimension of a madness or a *dérive* in which the event in a sense exceeds itself. If you just want to approach it in terms of 'correct usage', you end up with some appalling interpretations. Not knowing how to take an event in its singularity and its literalness leads to a kind of moral history-writing.

Especially when it is highly charged symbolically.

Then it's a very serious mistake. It is of course the easiest solution, acceptable to everyone. François Furet proceeds in this way, at the end of an already highly recurrent history in which the judgements he passes are very largely inspired by the current ideological situation.

There is a kind of denial of situation here in the Situationist sense of the term. And this has led to endless debates and rejoinders to them. For example, there was Stéphane Courtois with Le Livre noir du commu-nisme, *then the rejoinder to the rejoinder, as some tried to rescue the original position.*[11] *Not to rescue the event itself – that's of no interest – but the interpretation of the event.*

You could make an – itself interpretative – reduction of Furet's interpretation, given the historical elements we have available to us, but then we plunge into something we'll never get out of. We are in critical space and it isn't easy to get out of it either conceptually or historically, given the hegemonic vision we have nowadays of history. It's the same with the singularity of species. Each species in itself is perfect. The human species is perfect: there's no point perfecting it. It's bad, but perfect: in its singularity, it's incomparable. There is clearly a problem: in asserting the perfection of each species, you may lapse into creationism! The argument would be that everything was there by God's grace, unchangeable, etc. The danger would be to go back to a mythic version of things, but the principle of historical and mental evolutionism is just as dangerous.

We must give each detail, each fragment, each species its incomparable tonality, and not teleologize them as such!

4   Fragments and fractals

We accept the real and its self-evidence so easily only because we sense that reality does not exist.

Jorge Luis Borges

A feature of our age is its inability to confront evil directly. You say, 'We do not know how to speak evil any more.'

The great confusion is between *le mal* and *le malheur*, between evil and misfortune! The reduction of evil to misfortune, and good to happiness. The ideology of happiness is, in itself, an entirely unhappy thing!

In your view, the way we approach this today seems beset with pitfalls.

Some analyses are intellectually correct, but it's the critical form the acceptance of things takes today! Anything and everything is endorsed, in a critical way! That's the dominant thinking today. Debord was right about this. It's what he called integrated criticism, integrated subversion, with all these things spiralling around on themselves. We have to break down this kind of solidarity between good and evil, this sort of 'dialectical' complicity. We have to give evil back its radicalism.

*A non-ontological radicalism! To know whether evil is privation of good (*privatio boni*), whether it can be radical or absolute, whether it is sometimes in-itself or for-itself, moral or metaphysical, etc. – all these debates which will occupy philosophy and theology for a long while yet are not really your concern. The point is, rather, to conceive a kind of fragmentary radicalism of evil.*

Yes, you might say that, since it could be said in the end that evil isn't the opposite of good, because the two are asymmetric. In a sense the fragment is evil in relation to the whole, which is good. This brings us to the famous transparence or, more accurately, *'transparition'* (showing-through) of evil. Behind all our technologies of the good and of happiness, the driving force is evil! So, in the end, our whole strategy is one of treating evil with evil. It is the accomplishment of evil, in its homeopathic form, so to speak.

The aphorism or the fragment could be said to be a 'critical' form in the Hippocratic sense of the term, the 'crisis' being what enables you to make a diagnosis. A kind of 'replica' of the fracture in the fragment, and vice versa.

The fragment is indeed closely related to the fracture. Something happens in the crack in things, in the breach, and hence in their appearance.

A phenomenon in the strict sense, 'phainomenon' *(from 'φαίνεσθαι', which derives from the Greek word 'φόως', light), an 'appearance'.*

Exactly. It's in the moment when something is emerging that you really have a phenomenon before you.

One can then only welcome it, and perhaps record it. Hence the aphorism.

In the face of something emerging in this way, you can no longer stand back to judge; it is, I believe, of the order of becoming and metamorphosis. For a very brief period of time, you become that thing, that object or that moment, and then afterwards the dimension of being sets in again, so to speak, or at any rate the dimension of continuity. During this short time, there's discontinuity and metamorphosis. We have to conceive a set of rules which matches up to that, which makes the game effectively possible, which enables something to become – becoming being something different from change, and something that's accompanied by a loss of identity.

Which is also a loss of the origin . . .

Of the origin and also of the end. Until that moment comes which we cannot describe as total, since it remains fragmentary.

We're not far from the Nietzschean idea of the eternal return.

I was in fact thinking of that. In the conjunction of the two, the only eternal return possible is through the form of becoming. Is this the eternal return of the same? It can be argued that the cycle of metamorphoses is an eternal return of forms, but not an eternal return of the same. The point isn't to give scientific legitimacy to this idea, as Nietzsche would have been tempted to do. In the dimension of continuity things change, they have a history, but they don't metamorphose, they've no chance of returning, because they go off towards a kind of infinite. Whereas there are, it seems to me, a finite number of forms. In the world we're in, there's no unlimited potential, either of energy or of forms. We're in a finite world; the languages are finite corpuses. To say that the circulation of atoms will bring back the same situation is too probabilistic a proposition; we should say, more radically, that when one is in a finite world, there's a distribution of forms that condemns them to correspond to one another, setting up a sort of resonance, of elective affinity, which reproduces something like a fateful cycle, a concatenation, which means that one always finds oneself in the same situation, from one end of life to the other – what Nietzsche called character, which is also the profile of destiny . . .

The idiosyncrasy Nietzsche speaks of . . .

It's the fateful, *le fatal*. From the fractal to the *fatal*, to make a play on words.

Like fame or the finite number of souls. It's a new vision of finitude!

It's a question of putting an end to exponentiality, to proliferation, which is the characteristic of the world of production, for which no regulation is possible. To put an end to extreme phenomena in order to recover a finite destiny.

Setting the finitude of forms against the unlimitedness of production or its proliferation. We may, of course, mention Heidegger's Gestell *here – the technicist enframing or requisitioning of nature by the techno-sciences.*

Production is information. You have to destroy its infinite succession to be able to recover a concatenation of forms. The system of values that presides over all this can only aim for the infinite by a kind of contamination contemporaneous with our whole ideology of liberation. Liberation is, essentially, that. 'We must liberate everything' – it's the opposite of concatenation. Forms, for their part, are chained and enchained in a finite universe.

With a new watchword, 'Let's liberate ourselves from liberation!'

It's a great theme. At bottom, liberation is the process of good in action. If there are no other hypotheses than happiness and good, then we must liberate everything (even desire!). To submit everything to this liberation process is to disenchain everything and hence to open on to a de-regulation as far as the eye can see. It isn't a question of putting a moral end to this, or getting back to a happy medium, it's a question of finding a set of rules. The game is limited. It's a finite universe. It's defined by the rules. Outside it, nothing is geared to the game, and inside everything is subject to this rule. The space of a game is a singularity that has no other rule but its own. It knows no law.

You addressed this theme in Seduction: *'However, it is not the absence of the law that is opposed to the law, but the Rule.'*[1] *The law can be transgressed, but not the rule! 'It does not carry any meaning, it does not lead anywhere.'*[2] *You point out very rightly that when you are out of the game, you don't play, whereas when you're outside the law, you are still under the law. Law is without exteriority, whereas the game has an exteriority. So the game can be opposed strategically to the law, 'by choosing the rule one is delivered from the law', as you say.*[3]

Criticism itself is still subject to the law; the law is there to correct it, whereas a set of rules cannot be corrected. Here, again, one may be accused of archaism, of ritualism; yet it's simply a matter of getting back to protocols, getting back to forms. A form is a set of rules, be it the rules of challenge or of seduction. The 'rules of the game' are entirely immoral and do not correspond to a moral law or a social law.

So we might say more amoral than immoral, since we well know that morality can cope easily with the immoral . . . just as legality can with illegality!

More amoral, in a way. At any rate, they have to do with evil, in so far as that is what comes from elsewhere, what exists for itself as autonomous power, as singular power. And all these things can carve out parallel paths for themselves, alongside the official course of the law, of history, etc. They really are two different worlds! Happily, from time to time, they concertina together. Like a meteorite, a singularity appears and sparks a deflagration: that is called destiny. The mode of existence of these mental UFOs is really very delicate. But it exists! Running beneath the surface of the world of good, evil circulates everywhere. In exchange – exchange generalized into value – what everywhere runs in parallel is the nothing, the exchange of the nothing. There's a continuity of the nothing, so to speak, which is reminiscent of – and this is more than a metaphor – anti-matter. A sort of undetectable dark mass. This progression of evil doesn't appear as such; you can scarcely make it appear openly; there's a kind of impossibility of thinking evil, of speaking of it, or even imagining death. But this is constantly transfusing into all the forms of the transparence of evil. We might, at a pinch, say good no longer appears except as a site for the transparence of evil.

What was a great moral idea – the ideal opposition between good and evil, which long governed our ways of thinking – became the ideology of happiness (and not any longer the idea of good) and the ideology of misfortune (and not any longer the idea of evil) – two ideologies which are, at bottom, entirely in collusion. The misfortune is in this ideological reduction: evil as form is ideologically reduced to misfortune as formula. This is the easiest solution. It's a bit like what Lichtenberg says about freedom: 'Freedom can look forward to a great future, because it is the easiest solution!'[4] It's clear that man is not free, but to think this is quite a different matter, and few have dared do so. The idea of freedom is so much simpler and so much more acceptable. It's the same with other values. So, evil is enigmatic; it's intractable; we don't know whether it's original or not; it can't be shown or demonstrated, whereas misfortune is clear and can be delineated, etc. These are not things one can say because they're a challenge to the whole miserabilist pathos that prevails today!

*

When you speak about the exchange of the nothing, one thinks, of course, of Georges Bataille and the famous 'accursed share', prodigality and sumptuous expenditure: the living organism receives more energy than is strictly required by it. It is this excess that men expend in luxury, love or war. Something that goes beyond the anthropological underpinnings of classical political economy![5]

Bataille's 'accursed share', of course, to which must be added Marcel Mauss's 'potlatch'. But I found the idea of the 'nothing' in Macedonio Fernandez, an Argentine author who is very little known in France, even though two of his books have been translated! He wrote a very remarkable book on the continuation of the nothing.[6]

In which Bataille's influence shows through?

Not at all. It's much more in the Borgesian mode. And he was, in fact, a friend of Borges's. There's an absence running through things and this is the real source of energy. He's an extraordinary metaphysician, who doesn't perhaps have the same charm as Borges, and not his language at any rate, but is much more of a pataphysician than Borges was, with many a metaphysical *dérive*.

Bataille's Accursed Share is also a curious meteorite, a sort of fragmentary book.

There's everything in Mauss, but it's still very anthropological. For this reason, you might see his work as relating only to that sphere, but his way of having generalized it as a form is very remarkable. When I began to teach, I worked from three or four books – Bataille's, *The Gift* by Mauss, Artaud's *The Theatre of Cruelty* and Pierre Klossowski's *La Monnaie vivante*.[7] As for *The Accursed Share*, it really triggered something off in me. Yet it's a book I came to know quite late.

It's true also that you make a slightly different use of the accursed share, for example in The Transparency of Evil. *At any rate, not a functionalist use. For you, it might be said to be at the heart of evil and its eccentricity.*

The accursed share, as conceived by Bataille, is too good to be true, if I can put it that way! In an article on general economy, I outlined a critique of this sumptuous, unproductive, unreciprocated expenditure.[8] Bataille's idea still seemed too naturalistic to me: the idea of the sun as a perpetual source of energy. Well, it doesn't work like that! The sun shines because it is fed symbolically by sacrifice. So there's no expenditure without reciprocation. On this point Mauss is more radical. He's more precise. There's more pathos and romanticism in Bataille.

Perhaps also it's more religious in Bataille than in Mauss, even though he would have . . .

The most interesting concept in Bataille, it seems to me, is that of excess. In excess there's the secret of this metamorphosis we were speaking about, this possibility of a perpetual *becoming* of things. It's through excess that this little fringe of things passes, this portion termed 'accursed', if you like, although the term is quite ambiguous. If it's a reference to evil, then well and good. If it's a reference to cursing, that's much more of a problem!

Still this underlying religiosity. The pleasure felt at transgressing Christian morality assumes that morality is first taken as a norm!

There's a whole cult of the forbidden in fact. There was a time when Bataille was much discussed, or there was much discussion around his ideas. We were all agreed at least on the concepts of continuity, in the sense he gives to that notion, and sovereignty; all that functioned fine, but there was in his writing both a seductiveness of the fragment, of the rupture, and a temptation to reconstitute a whole, a cosmic continuity.

We should perhaps see this as reflecting the influence of Hegelianism, as recast by Alexandre Kojève, whose lectures he attended in the 1930s.[9] Even if 'inner experience'[10] wanted to break with systems, with the sequence of concepts in a homogeneous style of thought.

With regard to Bataille, and the others, you have to have a secret filiation, which has a kind of a silent efficacy to it. Researchers always try to find the tracks you've striven to cover up. There is, as a result, a perpetual misunderstanding.

Nietzsche, Bataille, Artaud – we're always coming back to these same ones. They're the basis of any analysis of the contemporary world and yet something else has happened since then, and this is what we have to look for. Perhaps nothing really crucial has happened. Or perhaps it has. And this is the gamble we have to take, rather than the opposite! To say that with Nietzsche, Artaud or Bataille we have the absolute and fundamental bases on which all possible analyses will rest can't be true. We have to find the event of modernity or post-modernity (the term is of no importance!) which, in its singularity, forces us, not to correct existing views, but to invent other ways of thinking, other rules. It's a wager of a Pascalian kind. Pascal says that, though you can, admittedly, get by without God, it's much more advantageous to gamble on the contrary option, and he shows us why. It's the same for us. We can live and survive with the real world, with the reality principle. That's what we do in a way, but it's much more amusing to wager that reality doesn't exist! If you make the assumption that reality doesn't exist, then everything changes, which is fantastic. It's true Pascal wagered that God existed, whereas here we're making more the opposite wager – gambling on radical illusion. It's the opposite, but it's also the same form: that of a challenge to reality, instead of a contract with reality.

And so, from a certain point of view, the fragment is a wager too.

Precisely. The fragment is a wager, not the continuous management of things. You have to gamble, you have to up the stakes. You have, of course, to think out the terms of the wager, and not get them wrong, but you have to choose between the contract and the wager (or challenge). The one or the other!

The social wager against the social contract?

But what is a contract I didn't sign, a contract already signed for me! If I want to enter into a relation as a personal act, that isn't a contract, it's a pact or a wager. This is part of the logic of any symbolic act: either you manage the capital or you gamble with it.

The contract fuels the illusion of a perfect symmetry on the part of the contracting parties.

There is, quite simply, the illusion of exchange. We realize today that nothing works that way any longer. Accelerated circulation, accelerated exchange – it's the breakdown of the social contract! We're only just realizing this now, but this contract business was starting to wear thin a century ago.

The contract might be said to be covered, like a certain whale you spoke of some time ago, with the seaweed of old journeys . . . [11]

And with shellfish, which today are obviously poisoned! Even animals have, in a sense, broken the social contract that linked them to the human race. Mad cow disease . . .

To liberate yourself from liberation – as you say – is also to liberate yourself from all the ideologies of liberation.

If you start out from the instance of the subject and its transcendence, you cannot but valorize freedom, the will, responsibility – all the notions of the same order.

We come back here to Lichtenberg, whom you like to quote: freedom remains, because it's the easiest idea.

It's the easiest and the most acceptable from the moment it comes into play, because, before that, the idea didn't arise. But it's another matter to determine how this idea of freedom emerges. It's a mystery. He also says: 'At bottom, let us be clear, man is not a free being; that decree doesn't exist anywhere. Man is not free, but he cannot or will not realize this, because that requires such self-denying intellectual effort. Freedom has, therefore, every chance of enduring for ever.' [12] This easy solution is challenged today only by an even easier solution, which is freedom's abdication in the name of a kind of digital destiny, assigning things to programming operations and organigrams. This new operator sets little store by his freedom. Lichtenberg also says: 'To establish liberty and equality as many people now think of them would mean producing an eleventh commandment through which the other ten would be abolished.'[13] This is very finely conceived. With freedom, the source of all the commandments is internalized; this is the source of absolute unhappiness, you're responsible for everything! There's some reticence today about using freedom in this way, because we can glimpse a certain number of consequences. It's Lichtenberg again, I think, who says that the characteristic use of freedom is the abuse you can make of it.[14] The proof that something is in play is that you can exceed it, and make a sacrifice of it.

Let's come back to the proposition of the gift and the counter-gift. Freedom is a kind of gift, a kind of present you're given. The meaning of the term, as currently understood, includes the idea that you can do anything and have anything, consume everything, transform yourself into anyone whatever. So there's no possibility of a counter-gift. Being liberated isn't without its problems. For example, when slaves have been freed, not all of them have necessarily gone along with it; some have even rebelled against being freed! That's a problem we don't want to confront any more: the accepted idea is that freedom is a pure gift. Including at birth, as a recent trial showed, where it turned out that a child should be free to be born or not be born. Liberation is a system of exponential deregulation which necessarily leads to a monstrosity. It does so because we've eliminated the possibility of evil, of reversibility, of a duel, the possibility of a response, and hence of a true responsibility. If we can't respond to freedom, sacrifice to it, in a manner of speaking, then we end up being stifled by our own freedom. Cut off from a dual instance and having lost their reference, all things are destined to reproduce themselves indefinitely. The clone is the being obtained when it's cut off from its specific human reference. It is, as it were, 'schizophrenized'; being 'liberated' from its own original, it can only repeat itself indefinitely. Liberty has become liberation, that is to say, a quasi-obsessive process of unlimited and extravagant repetition. Moderation [*la mesure*], by contrast, lies in a dual relation to things, in a relation of otherness.

The virtual world is the culmination of the process of liberty: liberty is no longer even visible, having abolished itself in its definitive fulfilment. There are attempts today to counteract this, to rediscover new constraints, to reintroduce moral limits to the possibility of doing everything. There's an attempt to integrate a humanist critique of freedom into liberation, but it's hopeless.

Having said this, the mystery remains: how can it be that this phenomenon appeared and developed with such intensity that we can no longer carry out the mental amputation or excision of this notion of freedom? Yet, if we look at history, at institutions, we can see how freedom corrects itself by an intense voluntary servitude, and that the two function well together. Has freedom ever really existed? It has doubtless existed as an idea, an ideal, in a sort of illuminist imagining of modernity, a kind of rather crazy interlude. The fact remains that it's very hard to see how it emerged. At bottom, the same question arises where the real is concerned.

We can wager that the real doesn't exist, a wager in the Pascalian sense. We can connect the idea that the real doesn't exist with the idea of the perfect crime.

Put in these terms – 'the real does not exist' – then it may seem ludicrous. There is a reality effect. We can come at this by way of simulation. This is the path I chose, asking myself, ultimately, whether the real wasn't itself a simulation effect. But what was merely an effect has become a principle, a jurisdictional authority on the basis of which everything is judged and rejected. The real has become a perfect alibi.

It's the key to the perfect crime.

Yes indeed. This was all put in place gradually. The idea of objective reality, for example. Against that idea, we find in philosophy – in Kant, for example – a serious demarcation.

The unknowability of 'noumenal' reality, of the thing as it's presumed to be in itself, not as it appears.

You can't conceive the objectiveness of things! This goes for qualities: what is objective blueness? There's no blue in itself; it's merely a term and that's all there is to it. Reality in this sense is beyond our grasp. We'll never know anything more about it. We have only our representations. If we've rid ourselves of the ambiguity of the world in creating an objective reality, then we've also rid ourselves of it by creating a subjective reality. Indeed, the two things go together: the real is also made up of this possibility of the subject representing itself as such. It's the interplay between the two that assures things of their 'reality'. The trap is present as much in the idea of the objective reality of the world as in that of subjective reality, in the deepening of the subject itself as representational being. In foregrounding transcendental givens, for example, as Kant does. These are the epistemological stakes of the whole of our modernity.

This illusion of objective reality has today reached a further stage, which we might address in terms of integral reality. What we have here, in fact, is a total hyper-reality, which no longer even has room for subjective reality, for representation. This is our new world – computerized, digital, virtual, etc. This integral reality exists at an elementary physical level, since it's the reality of particles, of segments; it's the analytic reality of things, in which there's no longer even the possibility for a subject of recovering a representational whole. We're beyond representation, or have fallen back short of it. At any rate, we're outside it. Objective reality was of the order of representation, being connected with the impossibility of acceding to the object itself (the Kantian 'thing in itself' or Lacan's 'real'). Here, we're in a world that does without representation. The system itself provides an effective, efficient, definitive critique of it. And in so doing, it liquidates any critique of representation one might make in the name of something other than reality – in the name of illusion, for example.

The perfect crime is the murder of reality, but it is, even more, the murder of illusion. It will never again be given to us to return to the idea of an ambiguous, undecipherable world; it will be totally deciphered. This is integral reality, which, as I see it, is entirely unbearable. At some point, there'll surely be a massive counter-transference against this total integrism of reality, which isn't even objective any more, since there's no longer any object!

You can tell yourself there's something radical about this virtual world: being outside representation, being beyond representation, and hence destroying certain philosophical categories I myself have criticized. The situation is very embarrassing. It's difficult to denounce a universe that has rid itself of the subject, salvation and transcendence. What can you do in a universe without transcendence, other than partake of this kind of dynamic immediacy, of effectuation of the world in digital terms? But is this technical immanence the same as the immediacy of the world of appearances? Not at all! So, it's radical illusion against integral reality. The 'classical' universe is encircled by these two; it's doomed to a disastrous collision, there's no way out! So long as the world was a world of objective reality, rationally conceived contradiction was possible and hence there was a possibility of revolt – which was a liveable situation. The reaction to the integral world will be one of violent denial. But what will that be, what will come of it? That I can't see! Goal-directed development is no longer an option, in rational terms, and we shan't be able to cling on to some goal other than that one, which no longer is a goal anyway. The world of speculation is exemplary in this regard: no concern for any goal whatever. If some day a crash occurs, what will remain? Perhaps debris – and not fragments. This is the case already. We're in a world of debris, of waste. Nuclear pollution is merely a tiny intimation of the problem.

The fragment as resistance to the debris?

We find ourselves, in fact, with the fragment on one side and the fractal on the other! And the way we're squeezed between the two is quite dramatic, all the more so as we no longer have the where-withal to represent things dramatically. In the face of violent events, if we have an option of dramaturgy, then we're saved, so to speak. The integral universe, however, is no longer dramatiz-able; it's de-vitalized, de-dramatized. We're confronted with the unsurpassable nature of a universe that has absorbed its own trans-cendence, its own image. It's a world in which things are stuck together, the world of the short-circuit between anything and its representation – an immersion in the visual. And indeed every image is absorbed by the world's becoming image. This is perhaps the gravest danger. There's a kind of diabolical meta-bolism of the system that has integrated every critical, ironic or contradictory dimension, fractalizing everything. Everything's on-line, and there's no opposing an on-line event.

5   Anthropological fragments

We have perhaps too anthropomorphic an idea of Man.

Stanislaw Lec

I'd like to come back to what seems to me the very fertile opposition between the social wager (le pari social) and the social contract. As if, for example, the best way of solving urban violence and violence in schools lay in a revival of the social contract. There is here a positively surrealistic gamble. As though learning the contractualist foundations of the state could solve anything whatever at a deep level!

The concept of 'the social' has gone awry the same way anthropology did. When the idea of 'the social' appeared, it represented a break with all religions, all transcendent orders; it had a certain radicalism, in so far as it was linked to society in action and the conflicts that emerged from history. And then 'the social' became an absolutist concept – even an imperialist one. It was then extended retrospectively to all societies and, prospectively, to all possible societies. At that point, it lost all definition. If everything is social from one end of history to the other, then nothing is. This is a disastrous consequence of all totalizing conceptualizations. Anthropology had already gone down a path of this same type, extending the concept of the human to all the societies which barely corresponded to it, which were, in fact, singularities that should have been treated as such. A certain form of anthropology did in fact treat them this way, introducing the weapon of relativism into the analysis of modern societies, and this enabled us to dismantle the universal or its concept.[1] The social contract functions to put a stamp on an abstraction, a fleeting reality. It was analytical abstraction that created 'the social'. At bottom, the same is true of 'the political'. What do we mean by this concept?

I tend, rather, to see things in terms of reversible forms, challenges, seduction. Now, nothing is more contrary to this world of forms than purely conceptual analysis, which passes everything through the medium of a terminology, a science or an institution. That way, you arrive quite simply at meaningless stereotyped discourse!

If I understand you right, the social is nowhere to be found?

So long as the social was merely a utopian, destabilizing, non-established dimension, it had a subversive value, but as soon as it became something established, even in contractual terms, things changed. Has the social contract ever functioned? It's a mystery. It functioned for those who drew it up, but has it really been recognized? And this goes for the whole of modernity: has there genuinely been rationalization? The social is like a hypertext that's been generating itself at least since the eighteenth century; it's sustained by intellectuals and politicians, being more or less their stock in trade. It's not that it's cut off from reality, but it functions on its own, like a highly perfected technical object. It's all there is left to refer to things by, so we no longer see through things – the black box of the social has closed again. It's a good thing that all kinds of phenomena are coming up which no longer fall under the aegis of the social. When the major events are unemployment, mad cow disease . . .

And paedophilia. Three events which are rather – as you say in Cool Memories IV *– anti-events, non-events.*[2]

Exactly. All events that are not fundamentally of a social or political order, but which people try to politicize, and to which political significance gets attached, like the contaminated blood scandal. Politics ends up revolving entirely around these things, but they come, fundamentally, from elsewhere; they are contestations that have their origins in biology or other sectors. To try to reduce everything to social conflict was merely a dream. When I hear talk today of the social or the political, I get the impression people are talking to themselves and between themselves, which may fuel endless polemics, but that something is left entirely outside all that. The problem began with the concept of the mass, of the silent majority. The masses are no longer social! We speak of them in terms of sociology, as though this were a substance penetrable by the social, rationalizable by progress. But it isn't at all. The further we advanced into the social, the more a kind of dark matter formed.

You speak of the masses even as an indefinable anti-matter of the social. The masses might be said to be inertia, the power of the neutral. And the silent majorities cannot be seen as conductive of 'the social', or 'the political', or meaning.

Yes, indeed. An entirely resistant, irreducible 'matter', which we have tried to pin down by opinion-polls, statistics, and so on, as we've tried to pin down chaos in physics by the calculation of probabilities. You then set up a science which deals with these things, which holds up a kind of mirror to the masses and the social. There is in this a total misunderstanding of something which is not an anti-power, but a silent potency – or anti-potency – standing outside the social contract, and belonging thoroughly to the order of the challenge.

We find the social challenge here once again, rather than the social contract.

It's another agency acting against the social; it's possible today that there are many energies preparing to contest the social. We only have to think of all those secret or mysterious ways by which people resist representation. This is obvious with political representation, which is being very deeply challenged, but it's also the case with any kind of representation. For better or worse, because denying representation – I don't need representing any more, I don't have to be represented – can be a mark of total sovereignty or the sign that you've been entirely overwhelmed, been scattered, steamrollered, and that you no longer even have any notion of yourself, nor any ideal to defend. Neither the politicians nor the intellectuals will face up to this state of affairs because democracy rests on this postulate of representation. Now, there's an increasingly great demand not to be represented, extending perhaps even to words, which might be seized by the temptation to stop meaning anything.

This could take us a long way.

There's a kind of relatively silent, unknown insurrection going on here, but one in which it seems to me that something fundamental is at stake.

To escape the power of language – in language 'servility and power are inescapably intermingled at the price of the impossible', as Barthes would say. [3]

Naturally, against language in the sense in which Barthes said it was fascist, since it is a summons to speak, and fascism wants to make people speak. People don't perhaps want to speak in that sense. Politicians are not all unintelligent, and doubtless some of them have an inkling of what is going on, but this is something they certainly cannot admit. I went so far as to suggest that politicians and the political class in general were there to manage this false 'accursed share', made up of all the waste-matter of 'the social' which no one knows what to do with, and that the masses (who are not necessarily millions of individuals) merrily fob all this rubbish off on to that coterie – or perhaps we should say mafia – who are lumbered with the filthy job and who are, ultimately, sacrificial victims. We need an analytical reversal of the situation. Not to criticize the political sphere, corruption, etc., but to ask ourselves if all this isn't a kind of opposite strategy, a strategy that's not calculated – and is for that reason beyond attack – in the sense that the political scene is tolerated the way it is (with all the secondary gains the politicians themselves can derive from it) because power is in itself contemptible! Now, a certain rationalism may have led us to believe that power was a desirable thing, particularly in the years when power and desire went together and represented a kind of ideal cocktail. And yet it's never been demonstrated that power – any more than representation or truth, or even good – was deeply anchored in the collective desire. Any more, indeed, than social being. As though the human being were a social being!

That's one of the assumptions of all anthropology . . .

Every effort is made to keep this absolute assumption afloat. If we cast doubt on it, how will things stand then? There's the same assumption with the news media and journalists, who are criticized for playing fast and loose with the facts, with exploiting events. And indeed they have accused themselves of this, repenting publicly. Now, if we admit that the news and information media are a sort of viral activity, we may very well take the view that it isn't the job of journalists to exert a critical function on the event, that their job is to provide raw material and leave people the freedom to use it as they will. That people should at least have the freedom not to believe what they're told, and to see the news media for what they are – namely, a spectacle, a parody, a pastiche of the coming-to-pass of the world, and not an object that critically provides us with information in the noble sense, or with knowledge. We have, then, to take media people for what they are, and not seek to correct or rectify their role, to put them back into some kind of objective position. No, they are functional and that's all there is to it. But I claim the freedom to be able to judge for myself, without collusive interactivity. It's they who provide the information. Well, let them get on with it! It's the same in the theatre. I'm quite happy to be in the auditorium: let the actors act and not take me for anything other than a member of the audience. Let's try to retain at least that sovereignty. Instead of trying to socialize everything, to interactivize everything, let's try to say: 'No, that's *your* problem; for my part, I'm free to decide for myself.'

To do what with that decision?

How can things turn out? That is, in fact, the great mystery. Let's assume that people have this demand not to be represented any more, that they don't want anyone to speak in their name – ultimately not even themselves, so that they no longer speak in their own name (it's an illusion to posit an individual agency of desire and power). What will become of us if we remove this hindrance? It's a mystery, but a really exciting one. What remains when we take away all these highly invasive superstructures? Naturally we aren't going to find a human nature. That too is a kind of superstructure. We won't find a nature in the individual sense of the term – but perhaps the duality I'm so fond of, the idea that everything takes place in a kind of attraction/distraction, where you can't pin down responsibility or freedom at any given point. It's a game! You have to keep to this idea that there's an insuperable confrontation and antagonism. And that we've always tried to conjure away this primal – and, in a sense, untamed – situation by the insertion of a representative space, a space that's rational, intellectual, conceptual, etc.

Any form of elevation, in the literal sense . . .

There is genuinely a question here. I don't suppose we're the only age to have run up against such questions, such an unfathomable radicality. The problem is, rather, to take the radicality into the very heart, not just of the space of representation, but also of this kind of fourth dimension, in which the space of representation is itself abolished. What becomes of duality in a space not just with three dimensions, but where a fourth dimension volatilizes all the elements of the problem?

*

When people don't quite know how to classify you – neither as a philosopher, nor as a writer – they make you a sociologist and, moreover, a sociologist 'by training'. Which is quite funny, as you admit yourself that you had no sociological training.

I don't even deny it any longer. But the habit does seem to have developed of calling me either a philosopher or a writer. What does it matter! Sociology should be called to account again, as I did in *In the Shadow of the Silent Majorities*.[4] I was, in a way, settling accounts in that book. The social provided a dynamic line of analysis in Caillois's time, for example, in the days of the Collège de Sociologie. It was a good angle of attack, though one which was not at all in the tradition of the social contract.

We should say here that Georges Bataille, Roger Caillois and Michel Leiris founded the Collège de Sociologie in 1937 – the 'college' developing out of the journal Acéphale *– to study the presence of the sacred in social realities.*[5]

It was something quite different from the representation of the social, from this kind of socio-therapy that sociology has become today. While remaining an academic object, the 'social' has imperceptibly become a parallel space–time, which you can no longer grasp, out of which whole categories have been expelled, being now 'extra-socialized'. The social will soon become an integral category – like integral reality – but there'll be no one left in it; it'll be a desert! And naturally, there'll be no contract here any longer, since there'll be no possibility of representation! On this integral social floats the curdled layer of politics, a vague coating of ice, a false mirror-stage, with extras posing as actors. On the other hand, the other universe, in which lots of things happen, is a split-off universe, a parallel universe. It isn't an object for sociology. Sociologists always hold to the idea of a rationality of the social, a goal for, and goal-directed transparency of, the social.

Together with the fashionable idea of the social bond – a notion dished up every which way!

Those concerned with exclusion never get beyond that: exclusion as misfortune [*malheur*]! You have to cross-fertilize this with the idea of evil [*mal*], to say for example that exclusion may well be unfortunate, but, as destiny, it's something else, it's something played out and lived out. There's a tendency to regard all individuals as passive! Pride, defiance, honour – notions that are perhaps too aristocratic and hence archaic – have been replaced by freedom and by another set of notions around misfortune.

There's a social theatricalization of the victim, who becomes a chosen, honoured person, a kind of reverse elitism which, as Bertrand Vergely observes, constitutes a new aristocracy for an egalitarian age.[6]

Today everyone asks themselves where they can find their niche in misfortune! It's become the only surface of the social. There isn't much glory in this! The social which, in its time, was a fine idea, has assumed concrete form, has substituted itself for the political and is now itself swallowed up by the cultural. What an unhappy fate the social has met with – and sociology with it! The path Bourdieu took – that of a kind of activist regression in the name of the wretched, is perhaps the only one for sociology if it wants to outlive its time. I find it curious, all those people who've read Nietzsche and the others, but nothing has rubbed off on them. How can you go on doing your own thing in your own little discipline as though nothing had happened?

I pity – a figure of speech, since no one is to be pitied, neither oneself nor anyone else – an intelligence that's always getting caught up in its own outdated facts, its own values. There's the internalizing of a discipline or a reality or a group; a siding with something. Then there's no cross-disciplinary outlook, but sheer immersion. There are lots of people who can live only fully immersed in something, a variant of protectionism. Without it, life would be too much to cope with.

All this has been short-circuited now, concertina-ed by technological change, which is much vaster and more definitive in its integrism. The state of confusion generated is very interesting to observe: as the whirlwind approaches, the century is going into convulsions. We have, in a way, gone beyond the end. People want to hold on to their goals [*leur finalité*], but they're already beyond them. They're living wholly at odds with themselves. They're living in a mode that's no longer the traditional, representative, social, electoral mode. The sham nature of elections has reached an extraordinary pitch – and not just in the United States! And I don't know what could take the place of the representative system. Maybe nothing! It's the consecration of emptiness, the emptiness show!

This is the image you use. Let me quote you here: 'What is there beyond the end? Beyond the end extends virtual reality, the horizon of a programmed reality in which all our known functions – memory, emotions, sexuality, intelligence – become progressively useless. Beyond the end, in the era of the transpolitical, the trans-sexual, the transaesthetic, all our desiring machines become little spectacle machines, then quite simply bachelor machines, Duchamp-style, before dying away into the countdown of the species. The countdown is the code of the automatic disappearance of the world.'[7]

There's a strategic use of this 'beyond the end', but it's increasingly difficult when the processes become exponential. To pass beyond the end is to bring into play the other arrow of time, to collapse the presumption of its end into the event itself. What would it be then? I've used this angle of approach a great deal, but it's becoming increasingly difficult to anticipate anything now, since the end is there without you being able to play on it as though it were a term set in the future. It's already there; we're already in it.

There's the penultimate and the ultimate, but not the post-ultimate!

Yes, there's the penultimate, the paroxysm – that is to say, literally, just before the end – but after that, nothing! We ought to find another 'oxysm' to refer to this temporal void.

6 Fateful fragments

Death resists us, but it gives in in the end.

Stanislaw Lec

Let us take on this problem of evil more frontally, the problem of its transparence. The idea that evil shows through {transparaît} and transpires, the idea of a kind of upsurge, of bursting through. We come back here to the idea of the fragment.

I come back to the opposition between *mal* and *malheur*: between evil and misfortune. We're in a culture of misfortune, a culture of misery. This is not to argue against the material reality of misfortune, but ideologizing it is something quite different. Ideologized misfortune has become a kind of emblem today, and a mode of action. There's a whole 'actionalism' of the deficit and the handicap, of legal action and seeking damages. The whole of the social order now rests on this kind of trading on misfortune, from which secondary gains may be derived. It's a way of rebalancing things in a negative mode, the mode of repentance.

We should turn all this on its head and ask ourselves what it is of evil that nonetheless shows through in misfortune, but is also warded off by it. The division of good from evil orders things. From the point where everything is divided into two opposing principles, in the name of which you can choose only the side of good, of course, we're caught up in a general trend to eliminate evil. This excluded, foreclosed evil shows through in the very system of the good, in the whole virtuous, pious organization of things: it shows through in the form of misfortune. It's a kind of resurgence of the repressed, though I don't too much like talking about it in these terms, but there's an almost physical backwash to it. What washes back is the old principle of duality and reversibility. The idea that good and evil are inseparable – that they're two opposing principles (all this is very Manichean) and yet at the same time inseparable.

You can put this in terms of anamorphosis: evil appears only in a sort of anamorphosis through all the figures of good – in their going to the bad. We're in a culture in which everything is going better and better and, at the same time, from bad to worse – simultaneously in two directions at once, like time's double arrow.

I take exactly the opposite stance to our idealism regarding the nature of Man. To the idea that everything is going badly, but deep down everything is destined to go to the good, I oppose the idea of destiny, which is the idea of evil. To side with evil, while retaining the idea that all energy comes from there, is a Manichean, if not indeed a Cathar, vision. Evil is at the origin of the created world. Though God created the world for the purposes of Good, he nonetheless ran up against a matter that was as strong as Himself, if not stronger. He didn't get the Creation quite right. Lichtenberg puts forward the following hypothesis: the world was created by a God who wasn't perhaps quite up to the job. A kind of slightly unsuitable, low-ranking divinity.

It's interesting to re-situate things in the perspective of evil and not of misfortune. And so to imagine that everyone is confronted with evil – in spite of all the efforts to ward it off and other fantasies, and is so even through their own misfortunes. Confronted, that is to say, with a form of destiny. Then human beings are no longer the victims of anything whatever; they are the actors of their own deaths.

Some time ago, I took part, with Marc Guillaume, in a seminar organized by the École des Hautes Études en Sciences Sociales at Lyon on the subject of road accidents. Everything that was said there – about speed, danger, etc. – was couched in terms of the idea that the behaviour of motorists is very largely irrational, phantasmatic, aggressive, etc. and, since it's irrational, it must be possible to rationalize it by analysis and technique. No one advanced the idea that this behaviour, even if it verges on the suicidal, is an action, a way of confronting a world in which anything goes, in which anything is possible. And that it is unbearable that all this should be given without the possibility of our giving something in return. We're speaking here of the deep symbolic logic of the gift and the counter-gift, which isn't an imaginary logic, and which doesn't have anything to do with the prevailing pathos around security either. There's a kind of passion for risk. It put me in mind of Palermo, where the traffic is a real dramaturgy of death, but well-acted and well-controlled: everyone drives to the limit, each driver defying the other right up to the last moment. And they do it very well, with the result that there are no more accidents there than elsewhere. It's a great game, and the person who doesn't conform to this law of danger is viewed with contempt! These are knights, knights on chargers . . .

One thinks of the 'agonistic' stage analysed by Johan Huizinga in his essay 'Play and Contest as Civilizing Factors' in Homo Ludens.[1]

Precisely. To speak of safety then becomes totally absurd! Whatever the dysfunctions, the pollution, the corruption, there's always the intention to find an ideal, technical version of things, an absolute reparation for this world which is such a mess. At the same time, there's a dizzying fascination in car-driving behaviour – a dicing with death. In a society where death is foreclosed, you have to find it somewhere. You just have to look at the daily soap-opera. What people watch above all on the TV are the weekend's road accident figures, the catastrophes. And it isn't that they're seized by compassion; they're in the grip of a fascination.

Michel Serres has spoken of a polytheism of human sacrifice, whose high priests officiate every evening on the eight o'clock news. And isn't the main part of television news built around the latest reports of death or sacrifice? Accidents, wars, earthquakes, epidemics, factory closures – all of them human sacrifices.

The political and social news that takes up most airtime doesn't really engage the imagination. People suffer that as a lifeless ritual, whereas the weather forecast, what the weather's like, what the road-death toll's like, aren't lifeless at all!

This brings us back to some of your analyses, particularly in Symbolic Exchange and Death. *Even then, you were looking at the question of the road accident.*[2]

Indeed. I get the impression people more or less consciously expect a blowback from technical objects. There's a game played with technology: it isn't just a medium; there really is a duel. We're used to talking about the revenge of objects, of 'Frankenstein' effects. This is very widely accepted. It isn't just accidents and death, but also technical problems and breakdowns – everything that both gives you the impression of a kind of ill will, but at the same time constitutes an event. A sort of breach opened up by objects, because everything today is mediated by objects or signs. Happiness or sadness, accidents or ecstasy can come only from objects – and this may extend as far as drugs or a psychedelic usage of technical objects (in particular the new information technologies).

Perhaps we can speak of a strategy here – like the one you talk about in Le Silence des Masses *– an offensive, paradoxical strategy or, at any rate, a strategy of collective or individual defiance of excessive security.*

It's vital to be able to respond in terms of defiance to safety, to the instinct of self-preservation, to ease of living. So there is no rational solution. The further you push safety, the more you push people into taking senseless risks. There are symbolic stakes here that can't be eliminated, and this is where the evil comes through. In our lives, doomed as they are to the ambient miserabilism to which all our superadded values of human rights and responsibility equate, evil occasionally breaks through, pours through, and we should let it have its head, not suffer it as misfortune, but take it on board as destiny.

This is not *amor fati*, but it does run counter to the general mentality, which is after all to internalize one's own misfortune. As a result, the transparence of evil becomes more refined: with all the means we have to do good (to create more and more virtual possibilities, including with digitalization, cybernetics and information technology), it assumes a very distinctly viral form; it has become virality itself, which is not at all an accident. We speak of the virus of information, but it's information that's the virus!

We may take up the defence of the accident, as a subversion of the order of things, but regretfully – with a certain sadness that the world should be accidental. Or, conversely, we may make it, not an ideal mode, not a revolution, but the opportunity to ask ourselves what would change if we took a different stance. For example, instead of regarding all the corruption on display in the political world as a kind of regrettable epiphenomenon, of waste, a consequence of the perversion of individuals or institutions, could we not see it as a mode of functioning? It's the functioning itself that's perverse, not the dysfunctions. It isn't corruption that's perverse, but order; and corruption is a way of pushing it to its worst extreme, to the point of parody. It's hyper-function! This hypothesis connects with the topology of the accursed share. What do you do with an excess? You have to give it, yield it up, expend it; it has to burn. Corruption is one of the ways of expending this excess!

One is, admittedly, forced to see matters on two levels: to have a normal, human, indignant reaction against 'scandals' and, at the same time, an analysis that's of a different order. But where does this paradoxical analysis lead? To nothing, since it gives rise to no principle of action, no principle of equilibrium of the order of things.

Beware of indignation, resentment.

What use is resentment, what use is indignation? Everything's there. And if everything's there, it's because we wanted it. There's an order of the will which isn't that of the will for good.

*

Where evil's concerned, you abandon any form of theodicy, of justification of evil. Your position is more or less the opposite of Leibniz's: not to stand back to perceive the perfection of everything, but to get up close and perceive perfection in the fragmentary. The problematic of evil is almost turned upside down: evil is perfection itself and not the celebration of good through its negative.

This is how it is with the perfect crime. It's the perfection that's the crime. What we have there is, indeed, a murder: the murder of evil. When I set out this idea, I remember certain objections, such as, 'What about exterminations?' Well, precisely, with exterminations, we aren't dealing with evil. Extermination is the extermination of evil done in the name of good. It's the outcome of a rational, logical order. The whole of ethics gets tied up in knots here: how can we act so that an excess of good doesn't turn into its opposite? Having said this, all things being reversible, there is an interplay between purpose [*destination*] and destiny. Perhaps when evil is pushed to a certain limit, it too produces good.

There is in your work the idea that the abolition of the real isn't the product of some remote decree: it's by contact that abolition is effected; the closer you get, the more it dissolves.

The real presents itself as a whole. The reality principle is a holistic principle. To eliminate it, destroy it, deny it, etc. isn't a naïve act, but means going beyond all possible wholes by a de-structuring. Then you get to the immediacy, the instantaneity of things and of their appearance. You go beyond representation, beyond the real. I've asked myself this question where images are concerned: there's also a murder of the image, or at any rate of photography, in so far as it's a two-dimensional world and hence not of the order of representation, which is three-dimensional. The image in the 'pure' state is a kind of two-dimensional parallel universe, which, from this point of view, isn't of the order of the real, but of illusion. The murder of the image consists in reintegrating it in every possible way into the realist order, into the logic of representation (the image as reflection, as testimony). All its singularity as a parallel universe is taken from it. A two-dimensional entity, like the image, is perfect in itself. You don't need to wait for a third dimension as a kind of complement, of supplement underpinned by a conception of a purposive goal, where everything added is an improvement. It's the opposite: all that's added cancels out what went before. With it, this two-dimensional world is sacrificed. Now, it's the universe of illusion, in the strong sense of the term, and illusion has its perfection in itself and isn't a stage in some process of evolution!

With the third and fourth dimensions.

The third dimension is a form of denial of the image. With the fourth, with the virtual, you have a space–time that no longer has any dimensions at all, a dimensionless space–time! I like the fact that the image is two-dimensional, in so far as that connects – for reasons unclear to me – with the idea of duality.

Your basic Gnosticism . . .

It must be that! It seems to me that the symbolic order is dual in that sense and that all the orders we know are, by contrast, unitary, totalitarian.

What you've said of the two-dimensional image can also be said of music.

Quite. When they began to build quadriphonic rooms – I'd tried them out myself in Japan – there was absolutely perfect sound reproduction, a sort of musical perfect crime. You had the impression that the specifically musical illusion, which is also a parallel universe, was eliminated. Sound was elevated into an object; in its perfection it became an object, and no longer something you can perceive at a distance. When you compare listening to an opera on CD or in a concert hall, it isn't really the same thing! The stereo puts out a music in which you're immersed, as in a bubble, whereas in the opera house it's listened to at a certain distance. The latter is real music; the other is a circulation in the mind. Obviously, you can be much more immersed in it with the CD player, as you can in the virtual world. And indeed it's virtual music: the more perfect the reproduction, the more it becomes virtual. Where is the real music? Who's to say? They've even felt the need to reintroduce noise and static to give a natural effect, or an effect of the hyper-simulacrum of the natural. At any rate, in the world of sound, as in that of the image, the quest is for adding new dimensions: triphony, then quadriphony, then multiphony. It's the same with images: they give them one, two, three or many dimensions. If you want to get right back to the essence of an aesthetic object, you have not to add, but always to take away. You have to take away all that's been added on in terms of time, movement, history, meaning or significance; everything that means that the particular spirit of the image is obliterated or, at any rate, masked.

Progress – at least what's called progress – always consists in adding on, in introducing refinements, sophistications. And it's more or less the same in the physical world; there too, hypotheses are added one to another in a kind of dizzying whirl. It's becoming impossible to maintain a system of values that could be called a normal dimension, the dimension of the real and representation, which is also that of aesthetic judgement, of aesthetic distance, of perception and pleasure. This three-dimensional universe has now begun to waver, submerged by a four-dimensional one, that of the virtual and the digital, the universe of what I call integral reality. The music we are talking about is the integral reality of music.

We can perhaps extend this analysis, by analogy, to the social, political and relational spheres. It does seem that, with the virtual extension of all available possibilities, with the airing of all problems in all sorts of alternative solutions, it's as if things are dissolving. What are we trying to do? Are we trying to fulfil ourselves more and more? This is, of course, the official version. Or are we trying to disappear, to hide ourselves away in dissemination? I really believe we are: the screen is a surface in the form of an abyss, not a mirror-shaped one; it's something in which you lose your image and all imagination.

The choice is a difficult one because we are forced to accede to this proliferation of images, to the world's becoming-image through the screens, the universe's becoming-image, the conversion of everything into images. But where everything is image, there is no image any more. No image as illusion, as exception, as scene, as singularity, as parallel universe. You can no doubt make the same analysis with music. With art, too, since what are called artistic objects are now situated in a dimension that's no longer that of illusion, but that of – more or less technical – performance, even if this brings colour and form into play. And even if the artwork is still a surface, it's now a performance surface, a screen-surface. It's no longer a surface obtained by the removal of depth.

If I understand you rightly, everything has become a screen!

Exactly. In the screen, the problem of depth doesn't arise. There's no other side of the screen, whereas there is a 'beyond' of the mirror. Which doesn't mean that all that appears as art is of this order; fortunately, there are exceptions. Every true image, every true photograph has value only as exception, and is, by that token, singular. Here, it's precisely the opposite, and continuous, perpetual succession [*enchaînement*] prevails. In integral reality, there are, in principle, no exceptions any more.

Which, by the way, gave me a problem with my photographic exhibition, 'The Murder of the Image', in which I exhibited series – in total contradiction with what I'm telling you. I only became aware of the contradiction as I was making the exhibition. After having spoken up for the singularity of the image, the two-dimensional world, irreducible to the three-dimensional one, there I was using series, which, for the image, is a way of entering the fourth dimension, the dimension of the fractal, and is, therefore, part of the murder of the image. Well, so be it. I won't try to justify myself. There is, I appreciate, a total ambiguity here.

Let's come back to the requirement to take something away. It's essential because at the end, so to speak, there's the fragment, which must not be confused with the fractal.

We must stress this difference between the fragment and the fractal. The fractal is a kind of segmentation, of proliferation, but each element doesn't clear the decks around itself. The frag'-ment really does create a void, a blank space. Indeed, that's what enables the fragment to constitute a singularity. According to Musil, the fragment is the smallest possible whole. Rothko says – speaking of his work – that what characterizes it is that it opens up in all directions and at the same time closes up in all directions. I like this image a lot: closing up in all directions. That, it seems to me, is what the fragment does. It closes up in all directions, whereas the fractal universe neither opens nor closes; there isn't this diastole–systole, this breathing, this rhythm of its own; there's just a continuous diffraction! Seen from close up, the fractal and the fragment seem quite alike. Neither is part of the world of the real and representation; both are outside meaning, outside representation, but they are so each in their own, completely opposing, way. It's a distinction that's difficult to grasp.

The fragment lies in the direction of anamorphosis, whereas the fractal is of the order of the replica.

Or of metabolism, or metastasis. You can make series with infinite differences, you can play on a gamut of differences, but it's of the order of the spectral, of the 'spectrum' of differences, not of the play of forms and nuances.

And then in the fractal, you find yourself again. You don't lose yourself.
A principle of identity remains.

The fractal is an infinite universe. In photography, for example, series are almost inevitable, given the way the technical apparatus simply wants to work indefinitely. Like the photographic act itself, which is potentially endless, you can't stop yourself. Any use of photography brings this possibility with it. Is it a danger? It is, rather, a dizzying whirl; here again a kind of dissipation. Every technical object bears within itself its indefinite repetition. The camera's no exception. So where does the possibility of stopping lie – not just of taking something away, but of halting the flow, the surge, of getting back to that void, that blank space, that suspense we were speaking of?

There's always a kind of hesitation between, on the one hand, the return to the one, to fusion, and hence to the ineffable, and, on the other, the temptation to go beyond the 'two' towards the 'three', the trinitarian, whether it be the Christian Trinity or the Hegelian 'Aufhebung' (the dialectical synthesis). As though it were difficult to stay with the 'two', in pure contrariety, in oscillation, poised between. . .

We must try always to maintain this discrepancy. Above all, we mustn't reconcile everything, but in fact, both in analyses and in practice, everyone seeks to reconcile principles. As Stanislaw Lec says, 'No one has ever asked the thesis and the antithesis if they agreed to producing a synthesis.' We must let the thesis live, let the antithesis live, and not try to move to a goal in the synthesis. You have to maintain the discrepancy, including in analyses, in the concepts themselves. Yet we always come to solutions of reconciliation or sublation [*dépassement*]. I do it myself. Language [*le discours*] leads us into it almost 'naturally' every time; we have to break through this again, reopen an antagonistic, implacable possibility for evil.

We have to stave off the dialecticizing temptation. The idea of salvation is totally absent from your thinking: there's nothing to save, nothing to hope for. You expound a thinking on evil which is not inhabited, even secretly, by the idea that there's something that might have been lost and which could be recovered.

Evil [*le mal*] takes on its full meaning in its opposition to misfortune [*le malheur*]. In its opposition to good, it's more ambiguous, as there's a quasi-romantic connotation of the term 'evil', if not indeed a demoniacal one, and hence one that has a religious stamp to it. The language of evil is, therefore, a very difficult one to speak, if you want to avoid seeming satanic, pointlessly satanic.

A temptation to which Bataille often succumbs. I'm thinking of his paradoxical adherence to the Catholic faith in the cathedral at Reims – we're back on your native soil – while at the same time vowing to subvert it. He'll never leave behind the will to transgress; he remains haunted by the experience of salvation. That is, more or less, what Sartre reproaches him with in the famous 'Discussion on sin' at Marcel Moré's.[3]

He senses the possibility of getting back to a quasi-natural order, the order of continuity. The order of a general economy, a naturalness, with the energy of the sun. There is certainly some of that in him. With Bataille, there's a theoretical vision. You have to take theories as visions, if they seem to be of that order. At any event, we should refrain from dissecting them to sort the good from the bad. It's true that there's always a background and references, but, at a particular moment, you have the snapshot of a thought, and it is what it is, whatever misconceptions it may involve. We should practise a kind of visionary phenomenology of concepts, rather than insist always that they be right or wrong.

7 Fragments and viruses

Propitious network winds bent their neurones
Toward the instrumental world's virtual rim.[1]

There can be no question, then, of resisting virality – at any rate not in the style of the historical struggles of modernity's heyday.

I'm a bit resistant to the idea of resistance, since it belongs to the world of critical, rebellious, subversive thought, and that is all rather outdated. If you have a conception of integral reality, of a reality that's absorbed all negativity, the idea of resisting it, of disputing its validity, of setting one value against another and countering one system with another, seems pious and illusory. So there doesn't seem to be anything that can come into play except a singularity, which doesn't resist, but constitutes itself as another universe with another set of rules, which may conceivably get exterminated, but which, at a particular moment, represents an insuperable obstacle for the system itself. But this isn't a head-on resistance. That doesn't seem possible any more.

We have in the past identified four modes of attack and defence, of offensive and defensive action, a sort of genealogy: wolves, rats, cockroaches and viruses. To begin with, the enemy comes at us head-on. These are the wolves, but the same also goes for human enemies: so you build barricades, throw up ramparts, build the medieval town; at any rate, you resist head-on. The enemy's visible. You know who you're dealing with. You might say that, up to Marx's class struggle, that was still the pattern. Then, following the wolves, come the rats. They're a subterranean enemy; there's no longer any way of defending against them head-on. You have to invent something else: a prophylaxis, a hygiene; you have to try to stamp out this more elusive enemy. After that comes another generation of enemies, the cockroaches, who don't move around in three-dimensional space, but in all the chinks in-between. Unlike the rats, they get everywhere. It's very difficult to keep them down. You have to restructure all the modes of defence. The fourth phase is the phase of viruses. At that stage we're in a fourth, viral dimension where resistance is no longer possible. What can you do then?

Sacrifice the supposedly pathogenic agents by veterinary carcase-burning . . .

We have to see what all this corresponds to. The rats are all the secret systems – intrigue and the like. The cockroaches represent parasitic action on all systems, making it impossible to be able to channel things. But the viruses are worse, because they are information itself. The virus is a supreme information-carrier, and at the same time it's destructive of information. It's an enemy, but we know nothing about it. Has it even a function? A vital function? It gets very difficult to protect yourself against it. These are problems the system itself has to answer, in terms of its self-defence. But those who wish to attack the system from the rear also face the same problem, since you have necessarily to follow the same lines of defence and attack.

In political terms, there are different levels: a level of head-on reaction and a level of subterranean abreaction. We have to make a clear distinction between reacting, which is to arm oneself against – and try to destabilize – the system, and abreacting. Abreaction consists merely in expelling something: you just don't accept it, but you don't fight it either, and you harbour no illusions about the possibility of overcoming it. It's simply unacceptable. This kind of abreacting seems to me today to be the mark of a very deep dissatisfaction, but a dissatisfaction that can no longer be channelled through a critical consciousness and is no longer able to arm itself against a visible enemy.

Against an invisible and hence elusive enemy, I suppose you have to make yourself invisible and elusive. Thought has to become viral itself. This isn't a pessimistic conclusion, but you have to fight the enemy with its own weapons, in terms of its own logic. What we need, then, is a thinking that, in order to pose a challenge, is a match for a system that's paradoxical, elusive and random. There's a lot of self-delusion in trying to force problems back into traditional moulds: joining unions, protesting, demonstrating, as though we were still dealing with the same old world.

In his last book, The Great Disruption, *which hasn't been translated into French yet, Francis Fukuyama says the Internet will rebuild our societies; after the end of history, announced by him, the information revolution will enable us to recover the lost unity of our workplace and the site of our family life (through tele-working). A new social order that reactivates the old one . . .*

The account of things set out in *The End of History* seemed relatively unobjectionable to me, except that it was viewed very optimistically, very empathetically in relation to the system itself. For me, the Internet is part of the problem; it isn't a solution. We might even say it's the core of the problem today. I don't lend much credence to ideas of conviviality or even tribalism. Or then you can stay within a tradition that's more or less that of McLuhan: his analysis of the new media – globalism, the global village – was, in its way, quite optimistic.[2] But he was writing at a time when you could still see, if not a glowing future, then at least an open one, because we were still in a heroic period where the new technologies were concerned. This isn't the case any longer. We're in a period of saturation, and it's one thing to be facing a wave and quite another to have your head under the water.

What is a thinking that makes itself invisible and elusive? In other words, what is a thinking which itself becomes viral?

What becomes of a thinking [*une pensée*] when it's confronted with a world that is no longer exactly the critical world, the world of crisis and critical thought? Has it any purchase on a world that has become virtual and digital? I don't think so. Thought must be both homologous with its object and must at the same time be able to mark itself off from it one way or another. In relation to a viral, digital world and the like, thought too must perhaps become viral itself – that is to say, capable of creating different chains and unchainings of thought from those of objective or even dialectical criticism. It must be both immersed in this virality of the world and, at the same time, stand opposed to it: otherwise, it no longer exists as thought. It's a structural contradiction, but it's also an interesting condition: what does thought do with its object? Should it reflect it in terms of truth, be of the order of disclosure, refract it?

Or be of the order of correspondence – all the modalities of traditional metaphysics.

Or, alternatively, must thought be an event in itself, something which speeds up the order of the world? I am, rather, in favour of a thinking which obeys the rules by which the world plays itself out – since, if it plays another game, it no longer has any purchase – but a thinking which hastens the course of the world, precipitates it, in the literal sense of the word, towards its end. It's a precipitating factor. Otherwise, it doesn't constitute an event.[3] Thought, in this sense, remains a fatal strategy; it is in the order or disorder of things, which is no longer so very dialectical. It accentuates this sensitivity to the final conditions which seem to me to characterize the current course of the world, a paroxystic course. Thought is, then, this paroxystic element that is just before the end, but is moving ever more quickly towards the end. It's a little metaphysical still. Thought might perhaps be said to share the physical condition of the world, which is viral, but it remains metaphysical in the sense that it shifts that condition to the second level; it ratchets up that 'objective' condition, which is objective only in name. What is going on now with thought is that there's a form of osmosis – though not of confusion – between subject and object, a form of chain reaction, rather than of reflection of the one on the other.

The epistemological break, so dear to Althusser, which gave a certain very French epistemology its finest hour, has had its day.

Yes, it's finished. While we were dealing with an objective reality principle, an objective reality, critical thought was within the realm of possibility. But if we take the hypothesis that we're dealing with an integral reality, an extreme reality, a reality more real than the real, a completion of reality that vanishes into virtuality, into the immanence of operations, we have to envisage other ways of thinking. This is very difficult to conceive, since thought has to be more and more radical, has increasingly to challenge the very order of cause and effect. In precipitating things towards their end, it's more in the area of effects (whereas critical thinking is in the area of causes; it lies always in the search for causes). This radical thinking, which corresponds to integral reality, is, then, in the area of effects: that is to say, it veers towards a form of paroxysm and extreme phenomenon we've already talked about.

But this remains very largely unresolved for me too, because this radical thinking has to be translated in some way into language. We come back to the problem: can language lend itself to a gymnastics – even an acrobatics – of this type? In any event, the advantage of this approach lies in its taking into account all the new elements: the random, the digital, the virtual and also the chaotic, which is the hypersensitivity to initial conditions.

The famous 'strange attractors' of Chaos theory, with the idea of sensitivity to initial conditions. To illustrate this phenomenon, use is generally made of the so-called butterfly effect. And why not? On condition that we recall, as the meteorologist Edward Lorenz reminds us, that, 'If a beating of butterfly's wings can unleash a tornado, it can just as easily prevent one.'

I have come to wonder whether the strange attractor isn't, rather, in the final conditions. This precipitation of things towards their end plays at least as important a role as sensitivity to initial conditions. Thought is doubtless part of the chaotic elements, and hence of the initial conditions, which as such are no longer causes, but it seems to me to be much more on the side of this 'fatal' final term – 'fatal' not in the sense that it might be said to be inevitable or disastrous, but moving *fatefully* towards an end.

This is, it seems to me, a bit different from the viral. Virality doesn't seem to me to be of the order of the fateful, even though there's something ineluctable about it and it's of a different order from that of the sequence of causes and effects. Can thought be of that order, can it create chain reactions, generate metonymic sequences to infinity? Doubtless it can, but it's impossible for it to be of the order of cloning, of viral proliferation. All that is really very difficult to conceive. I'd imagined this might be a piece of good fortune for radical thought: since everything is conspiring to transfer all functions to the operational order, thought no longer has to deal with that; it finds itself both released from its objective responsibility and from burdensome functions, such as knowledge or the search for causes and so on.

It would be an opportunity for thought to radicalize itself in a state of weightlessness. In the current disorder this is perhaps the option we should take. But, in this ideal state of disengagement, if thought wants to constitute an event it must also reapprehend the event and the new order of things – all these new strategies of the digital and the virtual.

We have perhaps to see integrated criticism and this precipitation-style thinking as running in parallel.

Thought has always to be a challenge. It has to preserve something of the order of the counter-gift: not so much a critical opposition as a reversibility, an adverse power in the literal sense.

Critical thinking seems to me to march in time with the world it criticizes.

In that respect it might be said to be heir to a certain philosophy. There was a collusive form of critical integration in which contradiction could still have a place. Whereas, now – with critical, contradictory thinking having in a sense been absorbed, swallowed up by the course of things – thought has to find itself another field; it has perhaps to move into this fourth dimension; it would then have a clear vantage-point on something which ultimately goes its way without it. In virality there's no longer any question of transcendence, and hence no longer any need for reflection; things unfold by a kind of automatic writing. Thought too must find a way of unfolding automatically, that is to say, in a manner predestined by its own end. The most plausible hypothesis is that it's the event – in the anthropological or even cosmological order – that's seeking an end, though not in any way a transcendent end-goal.

*

In Cool Memories IV, *you write: 'The rain which redoubles in violence before it stops. The water which speeds up as it comes to the waterfall. The athlete who "ties up" as victory approaches. Hypersensitivity to final conditions.'*[4] *And, in a more humorous vein, 'They say that old watches begin systematically to gain. Are they impatient for the end to come?'*[5] *What are we to say of this acceleration of the course of time as we approach the end?*

There is both a process which seems objective: things, such as water as it approaches the waterfall, go more quickly as they are nearing their end. This is a somewhat unfounded intuition which the physical sciences could perhaps verify. But it's also something I feel subjectively. A kind of hastening of things, of anticipation of their end, of precession of the event which occurs at precisely that point in their unfolding. A total uncertainty sets in, but it is part of thought itself. It's the thought which implies its own end; it's the concept which implies its own realization. There is a form of catastrophe here in the literal sense.

Thought must move faster than things, faster than the world. From a certain point of view, thought is preceded by the world which, without even hypothesizing an objective reality, moves faster than it. The economy moves faster than economic thinking. But perhaps there is another field in which thought can, in its way – by a sort of ellipsis – move faster than the system. There's the ever-ambiguous interplay of the parallelism and intrication of thought and the world: are they synchronous? Are they definitively separated? Must they be? There's a distance that determines a kind of unequal tempo between thought and the world. The 'conservative' type of thought, which assumes thought to be a reflection of the world, will always lag behind. It was Rilke who said 'Events move in such a way that they will always inevitably be ahead of us. We shall never catch up with them.'

This is the case with critical thought in its historicist form, its incapacity to think its object which always eludes it.

It's always the shadow of something. But there is the possibility of another form of thought [*une autre pensée*]. This is made possible by language itself: if we dealt only with facts, if there were only facts, thought itself would be of the order of the facts; it would not, then, move faster. But language is something meteoric, which may assume another dimension, find a transverse form. If you accept there's an objective world, you can hypothesize that it's subject to the sequence of cause and effect and that, as a result, it doesn't move very quickly, since it can go no faster than that sequence. If, by contrast, you accept there's an order other than the causal, of which thought is the instigator, a different order, in which the effect would precede the cause, in which the sequences would form and unform differently, then there's a possibility of moving more quickly. And, of course, it's that path I've found enticing.

Isn't the viral of that nature, as it is?

Yes, to an extent. It's another pathway that's no longer bound in to the causal sequence. Here we have to go beyond the hypothesis of objective reality toward that of integral reality. The same movement as leads from an analytical to a radical form of thought, which would be commensurate with a world 'veering' towards the viral, towards integral reality. Traditional, objective thinking is no longer up to this. What is? We come back here to language, to the elliptical forms of language, to the extraordinary possibilities for condensation – and hence for speed – that it offers. This isn't a spatial speed, obviously. Is it an acceleration? I don't know. Rather an ellipsis, a way of being able to concertina things, since language is not bound, in its literality, to the process of cause and effect. It can become almost a pure effect and, by that token, a sort of fantastic metaphor, establishing, by its speed, a form of precession of the event itself.

In any event, not an anticipatory, but a precipitatory form of thought.

Yes, a thinking based in precipitation and precession, not succession, which is of a rational type. The precessive order throws the ideas of origin and end into question; it overturns the successive order.

And hence, history and the traditional philosophies of history. This is the 'metaleptic' point of view, as you term it, which breaks with the rational course of things and stands it on its head.

It does. It's certain that language plays some part in this. There are perhaps other forms – why not? Plastic forms and sound forms. But language seems to me to be the major vehicle, the minor vehicle being analytic, causal thinking, which indeed we always practise in discourse. We live habitually in the discursive mode.

Yet the speech act, the act of thought, has the possibility of singu-
larizing itself, of taking an elliptical, rather than a syntactic, form.
It then manages to create singularities, mechanisms which no
longer follow the normal course of things, but can go much
more quickly, precisely because they have become singularities.
In their manoeuvring, if I can put it this way, they no longer
depend on the universal, on the dialectic between the universal
and the particular. They are something singular. The whole task
of art is to bring language down to its singularity, to wrest it
from the particularity and universality of meaning. This is more
or less what I have called poetic transference.

*

*You counterpose singularity to banality, but not in such a way as to come
back to the categories of the universal and the particular. This is also for
you the opportunity to go beyond the notions of identity, individuality, etc.
Don't you go on, then, to an – at least implicit – critique of the underpinnings of democratic ideology. An unforgivable step!*

I wouldn't fight on that ground; it's so ideological and demagogic.
Yet it's patently obvious that democracy, as Lichtenberg says of
freedom, is the easy solution. It's clear, he tells us, that man is
born unfree, but, for quite obscure reasons, he finds this self-
evident unfreedom unbearable. You could draw up a list of the
easiest solutions: reality, for example, is an easy solution. Thought
is part of a world it claims to analyse – there is an entanglement or
a circularity which means there never will be any truth. It isn't
possible to extract a truth from this cycle in which thought is
integrally implicated, in which thought is a fragment of a
whole which, at the same time, it mirrors. It will never be able
to provide an omega point from which it would be the subject
of knowledge! We are, then, in total uncertainty; this is the
non-truth of the world, the non-reality of the world. It is the
principle of illusion. The illusion is there, but it too is unbearable.

This isn't Platonic illusion, the lowest degree of knowledge.

And it isn't the argument that we can be said to have only a representation of things, as in Kant, and hence would never know anything of the world as it is in itself. No, the illusion lies elsewhere, in the entanglement and reversibility we were speaking of. This illusion is difficult to reconcile with existence. Hence the easiest solution: that of separating subject and object and instituting an objective reality. In a way, you can say that from the moment they are separated by this cutting of the umbilical cord, the object will fall into the grip of objective reality and the subject will end up in the illusion of his/her freedom. We are dealing here with a double illusion: the illusion of reality and that of freedom.

People find talk of this double illusion difficult to accept. You'll be met straight away with: 'What? Freedom doesn't exist? But you act as though you're a free subject!' Even if the sciences have reached the stage of definitive uncertainty, this easy solution, which has obvious, outward appearance on its side, is assured of survival. But it's a very exciting game for thought perpetually to escape the easiest solution. For want of being able to think evil and the principle of evil, we take the easy solution that is to speak of misfortune. Each time, we have this discrepancy, this gap. We have to accept this split; it's the extenuated form of duality.

Your dualism, as ever!

It's my transcendental Manicheism. But this duality is seldom experienced in its pure form. Most of the time it's experienced in the splitting of modes of life, of fantasies, of all the split lives, all the double lives, all the split societies which can be analysed from this perspective – the perspective of an abreaction to something unbearable.

*

*In symbolic exchange, as you conceive it, there's the idea of a reversibility
of terms: life and death, good and evil, masculine and feminine. A reversibility that doesn't come into the commercial exchange based on the use-
value or exchange-value of goods.*

This idea of duality is really crucial for me: it's of the order of
becoming. By contrast, individuality is of the order of change,
of a plural identity. Change and becoming are very different
things. Forms are of the order of becoming. They are never indi-
vidualized. Forms, qualities and singularities are beyond com-
parison. They cannot be reduced to numbers, multiplication
and calculation, whereas the individual lends itself immediately
to digitization and multiplication. And it's this, in fact, that
gives us the masses and the whole of mass culture, or cloning.
This gives us the fractal, if you will, since the dual relationship
has been fractured and, starting out from the basic unit, as in
arithmetic, you can carry out all the operations you like; you are
in an operational world. That's when you get into the series,
into serial virality, cloning . . .

Let's look more closely at this idea of becoming, as opposed to change.

At birth, one of the possibilities takes shape, takes *my* shape, and
everything else is ruled out; normally, from the subject's standpoint, the other possibilities no longer exist. But we may venture
the hypothesis that all these others, which I have not been, continue to *become*; I, of course, exist, but the others continue to
become, and, on occasions, I may become one of these others.
Not just the other selves, but the others-than-myself, with
which I can recover a dual relation, a becoming, not a self that
might be said to subsist through change. This alternative of
becoming can be seen in the notion of *'uchronia'* in the work of
Charles Renouvier.[6] *'Uchronia'* is the possibility of a retrospective
utopia, the idea that at a particular moment an event occurs, and
hence exists, but, as we were saying, existence isn't everything. All
the events that don't occur continue to become. Admittedly, they

don't take place, but there's another mode of being than existence, and their impact on the event itself – on the one that does occur – is considerable. So, what took place could virtually, so to speak, become something else, and did perhaps become so, and it isn't its end-goal that governs the event, but all these alternatives that we believe have disappeared. Their becoming forms part of the supposedly real existence of some particular event.

In the analysis of the French Revolution, for example, on which some historians pass an allegedly objective value judgement, we should be in a position to incorporate this *'uchronic'* dimension. There is a great and rather mysterious process of interplay here: the fact that, at a given moment, a particular decision becomes reality, a particular form imposes itself, to the apparent exclusion of the others. But the other possible outcomes are there. In the same way, perhaps, in the evolution of species, alongside a number of functional genes, all the others are obscurely going about their work. We should take this sort of simultaneity into account, a simultaneity not of the order of linear development, but rather of the order of becoming. And perhaps – we can see this as the Nietzschean horizon of the Eternal Return – all these possibilities will return, will occur in their turn. All the possibilities will then have the opportunity to occur and recur.

The self has its existence, its name, its history, and it changes, it identifies with itself, but I think it's always haunted by something other than what it is; it's haunted by what it could have become! This is very noticeable in poetic language. In Hölderlin, for example: his poetry is a perpetual becoming; he is successively the rivers he speaks of, his indwelling gods. He is not an identitary self, toying with his self-transformation into various figures; he is the theatre of the metamorphosis of rivers, gods and land-scapes. It's not he who changes, but the rivers and gods which metamorphose through him. He makes room for a universal metamorphosis.

In this, Hölderlin is much closer to Heraclitus – 'Panta rhei': 'all things are in a state of flux' – than to Hegel, his old confederate in the Tübingen Stift.

Infinitely closer to Heraclitus, in fact. I see here a radical opposition between a poetic, singular configuration, linked to the metamorphosis of forms, and the kind of virtual reality that's prevalent today. One can admittedly vary and multiply identities, but the (variable geometry) subject is still there. Whereas in the poetic form there's no subjected place; it is the forms which become.

We are, once again, as close as can be to Nietzsche; the idea of metamorphosis is very much present, and not just in Zarathustra. Metamorphosis and transmutation: a radicalism in action which, he said, will 'perhaps . . . one day be our posthumous fame'.[7]

Indeed. And this goes for language too. To manage to make language a site for the passage of forms, which it isn't in normal intercourse, where a definition of words and concepts persists; a site for the passage of forms, where words are no longer terms, but play-elements. Language as a kind of inhabited void.

The notions of singularity, destiny and impossible exchange occur together in your thinking. How are these three key concepts connected?

Identity implies difference. In the order of differences, and hence in the order of signification, of meaning, etc., there is a table of comparisons and exchanges. Singularity, by contrast, is incomparable. This is the essential point. It isn't of the order of difference. There's no general equivalent of singularity. It isn't governed by the abstraction of value and hence to exchange it is impossible. In each individual, too, there's something unexchangable, inalienable, irreducible even to change and existence. This is the character which may perhaps assume the form of a destiny.

8   Fragments of light

While resting on a summer's noon, to trace a range of mountains on the horizon, or a branch that throws its shadow on the observer, until the moment or the hour become part of their appearance – that is what it means to breathe the aura of those mountains, that branch.

Walter Benjamin[1]

Art which moves us all the more when it is imperfect, fortuitous and fragmentary – these are your own words. This is perhaps a good way into our subject.

The problem is, rather, the word 'art'. What are we speaking of? Is it still a category, a history? What we understand intuitively by the term 'art' today is what is encompassed by discourses, museums, institutions, the history of art, general aesthetics. But are there still works that distinguish themselves sufficiently from the general run of things, from banality, to merit the name of art? This is the problem. In a way, everything is aesthetic, cruelly aesthetic. But in the order of illusion, in the order of another scene, does a power of art still exist?

What you've written about contemporary art has made a great stir!

Yes, and it's not over. It's still going on, even on the Internet where there are sites responding, always in extremely vehement terms, to this famous 'Art Conspiracy'.[2] It's curious because, ultimately, a lot of people share this analysis, but at the same time deny that they do – particularly among artists and critics, obviously.

We could perhaps go back over this 'art conspiracy'.

What was I saying? First that contemporary art was worthless [*nul*]! That was a provocation – all the more so as I accord the term *nullité* another meaning, a magical meaning, virtually a sublime one. Being *nul*, being worthless, knowing how to be worthless, knowing how to manage the illusion, the nothing and absence – there's a whole art to that, and it has always been the secret of great art. Whereas great art is *nul* because it manages all the wastage of daily life, art has become – at least since Duchamp – this kind of automatic refraction of a certain banality, to the point of turning itself into waste, of managing itself as waste, but with all the bombast and aura artistic practice dresses itself up in. It claims, then, to be *nul*, to be worthless! And all this is accompanied by a certain blackmailing through nullity which consists in saying: 'I present you with such and such a "work"; if you don't see anything in it, then you are stupid [*nuls*]!' A blackmail the world goes along with, or at least that the majority gives in to. Just as artists work on the world or on their bodies, to condemn them to decay, to annul them, as it were, the consumer, the spectator, does the same work on his mental faculties, annuls them also, and it's in this complicity that true nullity resides. It's the conspiracy . . .

A kind of 'con-plosion' . . .

You could say that – a form of implosion and conspiracy. Whereas for me nullity has another status. Not everyone is capable of being *nul*; it's even extremely rare. Not everyone is capable of being mad like Artaud; not everyone is capable of being a machine like Warhol.[3] Contemporary art has turned its own disappearance, its declared self-destruction (announced two centuries ago) into its very material, but a material marketed and traded in terms of practice. Moreover, it has denied its own principles of illusion to become a performance, an installation performance, seeking to take over all the dimensions of the stage, of visibility, to make itself extremely operational too, and even if the torn and mutilated body of the artist is in play, this is still a conceptual operation. There is here a kind of forced visibility. With it, art moves into the same field as the media, as advertising, etc. It's no longer distinct from those things. Can we still speak of art? I'm not questioning the good faith of artists; I don't mind admitting that they do what they do in a state of sublime autosuggestion, but that cannot be the ultimate criterion.

Art has entered the field of consumption: not just that of the art market, but also of aesthetic vision. In the past (let us say until the eighteenth century) this illusion of art was not something shared by the masses; it was an entirely elitist object, wholly distanced, theatricalized. Whereas now, whether we like it or not, the masses have come into the game, and the artists have automatically incorporated this other, this terminal, that is mass demand. A demand that is, admittedly, elusive and improbable, but one that has been incorporated in so far as this mass destiny, this mass fate of banality, has been taken on board. Everything I happen to have written on this subject was the product of an intense, personal, subjective reaction, but also a reaction of annoyance and irritation and, particularly, of resistance to blackmail. That was what prompted it. Admittedly, you can find this same blackmail elsewhere, for example, in political discourse. If I singled out art, that was because it claimed immunity, benefiting from the aura its history confers on it. I took the view that this was a much more substantial abuse of power and prestige than you see among politicians, or even among intellectuals. Artists do claim a kind of extremely privileged status. So, no pity for them; we have to come back to what it is that they do. We see, then, that this is no longer any different from what people working in the worlds of media 'image' and performance do. The concepts of performance and information have, so to speak, killed the concept of form.

You say art affects us when it imposes its illusion. Now, contemporary art, as you see it, no longer is illusion.

Art isn't capable any longer of creating this distance, this other scene or other dimension, this alternative world, this parallel universe, which isn't 'art for art's sake', but a kind of challenge to the reality principle and to reality itself. Contemporary art no longer seems capable of doing this! There are many 'personal' exceptions, but as soon as you enter the field of personalized judgement, the polemic gets completely out of hand.

It's possible, in effect, that this form of illusion – and of myth too – is no longer the commonest form of art. In a way, old Duchamp – in doing his little cut-and-paste operation on the object, which is doubled up when it is transposed into another dimension – gave rise to a general detachment.[4] Since then, the illusion specific to the work of art has disappeared. We have to take this into account, while retaining the idea that it's possible for illusion to re-emerge in appearances, but certainly not any longer in the institutional forms of current art. Similarly, though the social was once an idea, and though the political was once a dimension, we aren't going to find these things in their current forms.

So, term for term, we might say that if art no longer moves us, this is because it isn't imperfect, but residual; it's because it isn't fortuitous; it's no longer unconventional; it's no longer fragmentary, but of the order of waste.

To get at this, let's take the example of the image and the photograph.[5] I've been criticized quite a bit for taking photographs and exhibiting them, and as a result being in art, being an artist, like it or not. Now, to my mind, the photograph, that type of image, is a form alternative to what I was saying about art. So I'm not too self-contradictory on this. Is there the possibility of a pure image, which wouldn't immediately be connoted by its aesthetic, by meaning, by the event? Can the almost anthropological status of the image be recovered, the magic proper to the image – that of a two-dimensional entity, as opposed to our universe of representation and reality – regaining, by that very recovery, a kind of purity? The term isn't a very good one, I agree, but can an image exist (other than a computer-generated image) that isn't the reflection or the representation of something? An image that would be – rather like what we said of thought in terms of the precipitating of an order towards its end – an accelerator of reality, but an accelerator towards illusion. An illusion-accelerator that is very clearly distinct from its object and is in a sense both an attractor and a form of destiny, of end. It's true that an image always puts an end to something; there's the freezing on the image, the freezing of the world in the image, and at the same time this definitive thing has already come to an end. What is captured is a form of objective fate [*fatalité*].

This brings to mind what Barthes says in Camera Lucida *of the young Lewis Payne, photographed by Alexander Gardner, waiting in a condemned cell: 'He is dead and he is going to die.'*[6] *A temporal short-circuit . . .*

There is in the image a parallel universe, a missing dimension which we should try to retain for it and so wrest it from the whole current visual universe, from the torrent of images. It's difficult, in so far as the same term 'image' refers to very different phenomena. How can we, then, restore to it this exceptional status of an image which puts an end to the world and is, at the same time, not its expression, but its emanation – a form of intuition from another dimension? To me, the photograph seems closer than film to the pure image. With the photograph, in effect, we remove movement, sound, smell and meaning from the object; we remove everything; the image is at the end of this indefinite process of subtraction. Whereas our common world of images is, rather, of an accumulative, informative order, just as traditional

; of an accumulative, evolutionist order. The other side is
active – I shan't say negationist – order, but ultimately
nts to saying that the 'real' and 'reality' exist only under
nditions, to which photography precisely puts an end.

*You say we must relieve the real of the reality principle. What is at stake
for the image is to free the real from this straitjacket of objectivity.*

Yes, the challenge for the image is, by way of an object, to quash
the principle of objectivity, and to transform it into something
else, which isn't of the order of the subject either. In the photographic act, object and subject have their own particular modes
of disappearance. You don't see many photographs today that
aren't already over-determined or connoted by the name of
the photographer, the theme or the style. Seldom do you see an
anonymous image. Some old photographs are sometimes beautiful
solely because we don't know where they come from; they come
from a world that is past and gone, there's no sign of where they're
from, no marks anywhere. It has become very rare to see photographs of this nature, and a successful photograph is one that
forces you to look at it that way. Admittedly, the pure image is
a dream, but the secret of that pure image has, I hope, not been
lost.

*We come back here to an idea you're fond of: photography as abreaction to
the world in its most unusual, most unpredictable forms.*

In the field of thought, I'd stood things on their head, saying: yes,
we think the world, but because the world thinks us! In the image
we find this same reversibility: the object which thinks us, which
surprises us, which makes its own way. Ultimately, it would be
best if nothing interposed itself between the object and the
gaze, if that ground in between could be cleared. I'm thinking
again here of what Rothko says – the idea of the work that
moves towards the absolute confrontation of the object and the
gaze, of the image and the gaze. At that point, it isn't a question
of asceticism, of sacrifice or abnegation; it's a game. The rules of

the game belong both to the subject and to the object, somethir is played out without the subject being in control of the game. Seen this way, photography isn't a privileged object; the same question arises more or less everywhere. We settle it today in terms of participation, interactivity or interface, which seems to me a complete trap, because there has to be a duel. A game is also a duel. Between subject and object it's not a matter of reflection or refraction, but, at one and the same time, a cancelling-out of the respective poles and a duality.

We have to manage to rescue this duality, this dual confrontation. The problem today is that, with the whole world having become an image, it's increasingly difficult to find that omega point from which to put the world into abeyance through the image.

Photography which, in your own terms, should reveal 'the evil genius of reality' in the same way as you spoke in Fatal Strategies *of the evil genius of the social and the object. Evil again . . .*

This is the business of the transparence or *transparition* (the showing-through) of evil. Things appear to us only through the meaning we've given them, we no longer have any radical or immediate apperception, there's always a kind of filter. We have to foreground the idea of a radical *'transparition'* of things, their showing-through. This may be the transparence of evil, but also other forms of transparence. We might say it's the same with the image: behind our usual, common and commonplace three-dimensional world, might there not be an 'infra-reality', another more subtle, more secret world which would be that of illusion and its evil genius?

A parallel world?

Just that, a parallel universe. But we may hope that there are points of contact, points of emergence and appearance. I think so, for if this weren't the case, things would be quite hopeless.

What breaks through isn't an additional dimension. Photography doesn't add any dimension to the real that might be said to reveal some unsuspected depth of the world or its real transcendence: the aura of sanctity, the spectre or phantom (why not fairies, as in Nick Willing's film Photographing Fairies*?). On the contrary, for you photography is a kind of radical 'fragmentarization', a real flattening[7] of the image.*

There's the intuitive sense that this world, our three-dimensional world, isn't perhaps as real as we think and that it perhaps doesn't need reality in order to exist. The image is an act of treachery against the reality principle; it reveals that principle isn't perhaps as solid as we think.

Many ethnographic accounts stress the thorough strangeness for many cultures of supposedly representational photography. You have to learn to decipher three-dimensional space. You've only to look at Pierre Francastel's remarks on the invention of perspective – a 'systematic space' – in the Quattrocento.

The advantage of the image in this regard is that it casts absolute doubt on this dimension of meaning, this third dimension that is mental and gives us an illusion of reality. I once read a remarkable book called *Flatland*, written by Edwin A. Abbott, an American author, in 1884. In it he first describes 'Pointland', a dimensionless world which is reduced to a point and hence to an elusive, uninhabitable singularity, but which takes itself, nonetheless, for God. Then comes 'Lineland', into which the narrator makes a foray – a one-dimensional world that's purely linear. Then 'Flatland' with the two dimensions of a flat universe. And lastly 'Spaceland', the three-dimensional universe we know. Beyond this, the worlds no longer have names and no one visits them yet.

The following thought occurred to me. Space had in theory three dimensions, then Einstein came along and added a fourth: time. But time itself has three dimensions: present, past and future. Religion added eternity, but God himself has three dimensions: Father, Son and Holy Spirit . . . so what then would the fourth dimension of God Himself be? The principle is that each supplementary dimension cancels out the others, and the fourth dimension – as it happens, that of the image in relation to the real world – would cancel out the objective conditions of this world. Admittedly, it isn't very scientific, but it's an intuition Abbott's book embodies strikingly. Everything that enables us to attribute a cause, an origin or an end to things comes from our being within the co-ordinates of a supposedly 'objective' world. So many postulates which can and must be questioned. The image is a kind of metaphor for this, and that's why photography excited me. I couldn't any longer see how to operate in the order of theoretical thinking. In the analytical field, whatever you do, you're always in the order of discourse, which is an order that's familiar, almost too familiar even – which carries away meaning. Whereas the image corresponded to a stranger rupture, a more radical vanishing point [*point de fuite*].

You also imply that there's no possible affective transference on to reality other than through a counter-transference from the image, and you add that this latter has to be resolved.

This may seem a bold proposition. But you can easily see – I experienced this myself at a photojournalism festival – the indifference of people's reactions to all the bloody scenes of murder and catastrophe of all kinds. There's a problem here, as there's a widespread illusion that you have to bear witness in order to bring about raised awareness. Not at all. Sensibility is completely nullified by the pornographic impact of the image! There is, literally, a murder of the image, a short-circuiting by signification, which means that the image itself, this kind of radical otherness, no longer exists as such. When it exists, when this transference on to the image itself exists, which is a counter-transference to the signification of the image, then something of what it attempted to signify does show through, as an added extra, so to speak.

Like the cure in psychoanalysis which, as Lacan put it, always came as something extra.

Exactly, it can only come as something extra. You can't pick up meaning frontally; an image that offers it to you that way won't be received. That creates a non-differentiation of meaning. For something like a signification or message to appear, the medium – in this case, the image – has to exist in a specific way of its own, to exist in itself; then we shall perhaps get a meaning. Otherwise, we get nothing. If we sacrifice the image, the meaning we thought we were getting through won't get through. There is here a form of paradox most photographers neglect. I was able to see this at Perpignan:[8] all the problems of a professional order relating to the right to the image, all these inextricable conflicts, came from the fact that they hadn't even posed this problem. In the way photography operates, you find practices that look a bit like the art conspiracy: between the photographic agencies, the dealers and the public, the information market is so circular that there's no longer any way out.

The same problem arises in language itself. If language doesn't exist in its own right, if we don't take it in its materiality, its literalness, and treat it in its form, then all that it's trying to suggest to us, to signify to us, fails to get through. This is a very topical problem; we're in this catastrophe of meaning, this total non-differentiation that's linked to an exponential build-up of messages. There is then a kind of zero-sum equation.

I like photographs because they're fragments, the smallest possible form of the whole. It's undoubtedly a very limited field but, here at least, you can try to see what remains of the possibility of the pure image – at least of its concept – and perhaps even of a 'beyond' of the image.

Your photos don't call forth any commentary. Otherwise we'd be back at an accumulative, evolutionist logic. You might say of the photographic image what Barthes said of the theatre: there is the being-there[9] of the image, and that's all there is to it: all the rest is literature.

Indeed. I'm talking about photography in general. Where each individual photograph is concerned, there's nothing to say, since it's a site of disappearance of the subject and meaning.

And you haven't yet written a book on your photography.

When I say I'm not a photographer, it's in that sense, because I can see that photographers want to be photographers: they make a product that is photography. Whereas for me photography's a medium. It's certainly a medium revealing of something, but it remains in itself an impersonal object. What interests me is the object, not the photographic project.

Those who read you from the early days surely didn't expect to find you doing this! They might have thought your criticism of representation would include photographic representation.

Indeed, there can be no question of successfully demonstrating that the image – in the sense in which I mean it – isn't of the order of representation. If one could just manage to give a sense of this, then that would already be an achievement. In the same way as I posed the question whether thought could move beyond meaning and truth, one may wonder whether the image and the photograph can also move beyond representation.

That is the sovereign hypothesis, the radical hypothesis. The commonest hypothesis is that they are both earmarked for the same destiny – for thought the destiny of saturating the discursive space, for the image the destiny of saturating the visual space.

Does your activity as a photographer owe anything to Roland Barthes, to the work he devoted to photography, Camera Lucida? *Although he wasn't a photographer himself, and that's quite a substantial difference from you. On the other hand he did draw, somewhat in the style of Michaux.*[10] *This brings to mind what Cocteau said: 'Drawing is writing tied and untied differently.'*

As it happens, I have one of those drawings, and you're right, it isn't unlike a Michaux, I find it very beautiful. A friend of Barthes's has a very fine collection of them which he exhibited at Rio. To come back to *Camera Lucida*, which I read with admiration, the book had no direct photographic influence on me, since it appeared in 1979, not long before his death, at a time when I wasn't at all interested! I came to photography in a much more occasional and fortuitous way, and only later. But Barthes's text was there and it's a permanent counterpoint or *contrapunctum*, Barthes being the one who used the word *punctum* to refer to the absent site at the heart of the image that gives it its force.

There's also Walter Benjamin, whom we've already spoken about, and his famous 'A Small History of Photography', which has just been republished in French. There, for example, we find the reference to an article in the Leipziger Stadtanzeiger *at the end of the last century, in which a journalist condemned photography as a black art from France that tries to 'capture fleeting mirror images', which can only be 'blasphemous'.*[11]

What Benjamin wrote on photography is key. I discovered him at the time I was talking about objects, images and signs, through his essay 'The Work of Art in the Age of Mechanical Reproduction'. I didn't then know his writings on history, which I read later. Everything he wrote seems to me to be extremely lucid! He cast the dimension of the original into question outstandingly well, and not in a trivial way. Admittedly, by talking about the way technology changed that, but even more by talking about the metaphysic underlying technology. I'm thinking in particular about what he said of the *aura* as being 'the unique appearance of a distance, however close it may be'.[12] He also questioned the concept of history. He was a pioneer in his day. And then he writes densely and poetically. But he's never been such a close reference for me as Barthes, for example.

Benjamin wrote some very good pieces on photography. He says, for example, that photography 'overturns the fundamental character of art'.[13]

It puts an end to its transcendent character. But he is very ambiguous on this question and I like that too. This is his modern, topical side, in the sense that he doesn't do timeless philosophy. He's always fascinated and at the same time repelled by what he describes. The object is always dual. We're not talking about an object that's been isolated so that it can be mastered in the analysis. You have the impression, rather, that the object wrestles beneath his pen; it's drawn in, it pushes him away. He's fascinated by the photographic world, as he is by modernity, whether it be the Paris arcades or the city. He showed an interest in almost everything. Finding the secret of a reversibility of writing, between what it says and the way it says it: the secret of a reversibility of history, which isn't linear. It doesn't run in one direction. Not long after the discovery of relativity he was perhaps the first to have translated it into thought. Into ideas, I'm not so sure, nor into facts either . . . but certainly into thought. What Benjamin produced really was thinking [*une pensée*]! We might make a distinction between a philosopher, an ideologue and a thinker, even if this last term is a bit too serious. Thinking [*La pensée*] is something else, it's an entirely unfinished vision.

Thinking that can't be said to be inhabited by an ambition to achieve closure.

Quite the reverse, in thinking everything bursts through. So far as photography is concerned, lots of things have happened since, but, ultimately, we've never yet resolved how things stand with the image in a world where repetition, the serial and the visual have a hold of things. It's the irruption of the democracy of the gaze into a world in which not everything was perceptible, not everything was worthy of being seen. Most things did not reach the perceptible realm. Now, suddenly, everything comes into that realm and this is a real revolution. And indeed Benjamin sees it as such. But sadly revolutions aren't as we imagine them, or they aren't what they were. He nonetheless gave culture a dimension that's not elitist, but rather qualitative, incomparable, singular, which must not be sacrificed.

An aristocratic conception of culture.

Aristocratic is the word! While being hypersensitive to all that's going on around him. In that respect he is, in the field of culture, to some degree the heir of Tocqueville. His status as an exile, as a Jew perhaps, gives him additionally this tragic dimension in relation to his own culture. Which is no longer the case today, with culture being perceived merely as a consensual medium, a great means of integration. In this sense, he was one of the great men of culture, without this assuming the aspect of a philosophical system. Moreover, many of his texts are like fragments; they are at best essays, always very short. It was this which, at a later stage, attracted me most to him: the form his thought takes. It's elliptical, a snapshot as we might say, reflecting a world that has definitively lost its cohesion, its *aura*. Must we, like the angel, advance facing backwards?[14]

Benjamin's work is both tinged with a deep melancholy – which is a quality – and a very remarkable intellectual adventurousness. This is an exceptional combination.

Among the many essays devoted to photography, we should also cite the very remarkable ones by Susan Sontag – in particular, On Photography.[15]

Certainly Susan Sontag, whom I read with great interest, or Wilhem Flusser, who's concerned more with the technical level. There are, like this, a number of outstanding books, some that are even a little mad, such as *La Photographie et le néant* written by an academic from Louvain, a kind of extraordinary mishmash where Benjamin, Barthes and Deleuze are all brought in,[16] a range of very good quotations, but also a totally fixed position, in which photography is seen as the absolute denial of the real, a denial both of representation and the real, and hence in a way as a symbolic murder. A symbolic murder effected by way of a technical object. There's also a murder of the image, in the sense that it's exploited for all sorts of parasitic ends, but isn't this violence done to the image a payback for the symbolic murder the image itself perpetrates on the real?

A murder with a weapon that's more or less Lichtenberg's knife with no blade and no handle – the camera with no blade and no handle.

It's what happens in the fable of the invisible man: if he touches a visible object he makes it invisible. This is true of thought [*la pensée*], which has, itself, a handle and a blade. Or, rather, thought has to be this invisible, indiscernible blade that turns around against the handle (the world, the powers that be?), which is itself non-existent and indiscernible.

It had crossed my mind that the ultimate phase of photography, which has never for me been an end in itself, but merely a line of progression, might be – as with writing indeed – permanent silence.

That would enchant all those who are absolutely attached to your Zen side!

That has nothing to do with it. The ultimate stage would be to travel through an entire country without a camera, and also without the slightest remorse for the lost images. In short, to go beyond photography and see things as if they had themselves already passed beyond the image, as if you'd already photographed them in a previous life. Perhaps indeed we've already passed through the image-stage, as though it were a stage of animal development of which the mirror-stage is merely the pale reverberation in our individual lives. Admittedly, there's no compulsion to get to that point, but I'm attached to this idea that, at a given point, a symbolic activity – be it writing or photography – can have passed into fact, passed into the world as it is, and consequently no longer has any need to exist. But for that you have to attain a wisdom I don't possess! It's very tempting all the same, whether it be Rimbaud-like, where you say 'I've shown what I can do. Goodbye. It's over!' – that was a temptation for a whole generation – or a form closer to disappearance, an art of disappearance, which wouldn't be *ressentiment*, but acceptance of the world as it is, seeking from that point on to remove all that intervened to disturb the play of appearances – that so rare and precious space of appearances. But, and this is perhaps good fortune, we're in a world that's too turbulent for that. It's too abstract a stance. I believe you have to be in the game while, at the same time, being in an offside position, so to speak!

*

In Impossible Exchange, *you devoted a chapter to photography as 'light writing', from the Greek etymology of the word, φóως γράφειν. What kind of insight does this give us into your practice of photography?*

The term 'writing' is metaphorical here. We should speak, rather, of light 'graphics'. When the word was invented in the nineteenth century, it had that meaning.[17]

You sum this up in an aphorism: 'Objects are merely a pretext for the light; if there were no object, light would circulate endlessly and we wouldn't even perceive it. If there were no subject, the circulation of thought would be infinite and there wouldn't even be an echo of it in consciousness. The subject is that on which thought halts in its infinite circulation, that against which it is reflected, and the object is that on which light halts, that which reflects it. So, photography is the automatic writing of light.'

Ultimately, it isn't we who grasp a part of the world; we are merely the obstacle against which light breaks. It's as ever the idea that there's a thinking that's independent of the subject: we think the world, but the world thinks us. There's nothing mystical in this, there's a gigantic process, and we shouldn't claim – we who are a spark, a fragment – to have brought it into the world. Thought, like light, is merely a phase in this process. In the cosmos there are two great mutations: the one in which it divides in such a way that light appears and the world becomes visible to itself, which it wasn't previously. Thought is the other great mutation, by which the species and the world become, if not intelligible, at least self-reflexive.

We are merely fragments, but at the same time we have an essential role: that of being there, of arresting light, arresting thought in a freeze-frame. We're the pivot, the *punctum*, which gives us a crucial role. I come back to the proposition from which I started out when I was working on the object: it's the world which thinks us, it's the object which thinks us. A kind of reversion that might be said to translate reversibility into terms that are, unfortunately, still alternative, because discourse forces us to say it that way. We should be able to express this reversible form in one and the same figure, in terms of a kind of poetic situational transference.

But not the 'Apollinian' light as clarity, as transparency, the one that metaphorically accompanies all Western thought, as soon as it pretends to an adequate knowledge of its object. Nor Bataille's sun either, the inexhaustible reserve of energy. It would be, rather, a light that casts shadow. 'But to give light implies/No less a sombre moiety of shade', as Valéry says.[18]

Of course. It isn't Apollinian 'brightness'. Nor is it Bataille's sun – energy without anything given in return – since there's reciprocation here. If we weren't there, there'd be no *becoming* of light, or of thought. It's thanks to us that these things *become*, but the basic flow, the basic energy, comes from elsewhere.

The light from elsewhere. Watch out, they're going to think you've received illumination!

There isn't exactly a source, but light proceeds, nonetheless, from a fracture in the cosmic order. In the beginning it wasn't there. This fracture created something like matter and anti-matter. The anti-matter exiled into cosmic space by the distinguishing-out of matter doesn't for all that cease to exist. It's this kind of dark continent that doubtless also radiates out. A radiation of anti-matter to which we might be said to be exposed and which makes us 'black bodies'.[19] Let's hope so! We aren't just instruments of light!

Where contemporary art is concerned – this is perhaps what makes it useless, preposterous and uninteresting in my view – it seems to me that no light appears in it any more. There are light sources, but no light any longer, except in a few cases, such as Hopper or Bacon. With a great deal of photography it's the same. What remains of light in a world of electricity? But the contrast between the two is itself fascinating. I was, for example, very sensitive to the magical opposition there is between the world of artificial light of Las Vegas – the world of gambling, in the harshly lit catacombs of the casinos – and the solar light of the surrounding desert.

9   Fragment fragments

He who has no shadow is merely the shadow of himself.

Isn't one always in a way faithful to one's youth? To what early thought or gesture have you remained faithful?

Doubtless to the idea of a break, a violent break, Rimbaud-like if you will, following a forced, very rapid process of assimilation during my adolescent years, a frenzied form of memory, all of which reached a critical mass. That break was to be combined with an intellectual and social break. Everything started there, it seems to me. At bottom, this has never changed, except that I put an end to the accumulative dimension, or it went underground, grew much more silent and hence less effective. Must one look in one's biography for the deep reasons for this break? Perhaps. I'm reluctant to sociologize, but it's true there was the break with my family, with my parents who were of peasant stock, with a largely uneducated milieu, to be propelled – by some obscure fantasy of my parents themselves, which I don't claim to understand – into a more cultivated dimension. But I've always remained deeply faithful to this primitive unsophistication. Culture is an added extra. It's something you must be able to reject, eliminate, do without. It's something other than culture that counts.

'He who speaks of himself should never say the whole truth; he should keep it secret and divulge only fragments.' This rule of scrupulous fragmentization out of a sense of delicacy applies as much to the theoretical and conceptual universe as to the real world. One should divulge only fragments and keep the rest secret. This is Kierkegaard's principle of 'scrupulous delicacy', to which I would happily add the principle of unscrupulous delicacy, of unscrupulous discretion.

*

Happiness is the easiest solution

Just as freedom forces itself upon us as the easiest solution to the problem of the subject and his/her destiny, so happiness has forced itself upon us as the easiest solution to the problem of evil. Or rather it is unhappiness and misfortune, even easier to manage than happiness, that is the solution to the problem of evil.

Just as freedom ends in integral liberation and, in abreaction to this, in a new servitude, so the unacceptable idea of integral happiness leads on to an entire culture of misfortune, a victim culture, a culture of recrimination, repentance, denunciation and miserabilist compassion.

We go on discarding freedom and happiness in every way, while continuing to speak in their name; we go on dreaming of perfect happiness, while sensing the potential boredom of paradise. But without waiting for paradise we are already confronted, in the form of an out-and-out technical culture, with the ideal conditions of life, and it is from hypersensitivity to these final conditions that, here and now, we are abreacting violently and obscurely, and are inclining towards misfortune and unhappiness as the most durable solution – a kind of 'cruise control' or line of flight – in the face of the terroristic happiness conspiracy.

We are not, for all this, getting any nearer to evil or the essence of evil. Quite the reverse. It is indeed misfortune that is most distinctly opposed to evil and the principle of evil, of which it is the denial (a fatal strategy?).

'For we know what Hell is like and those burning there, since Hell is not being able ever to do anything but evil. But what about those who, in Paradise, will no longer have any idea of Evil? God alone knows what awaits them.'

The unbearability of Evil

'Bis Gottes Fehl hilft', says Hölderlin, 'Until God's absence helps.' The death of God is, in fact, a piece of good fortune. It is the end of transcendence, the deliverance from all responsibility to another world. Henceforth the world is there, immanent; the world is totally self-evident and this self-evidence is unbearable. This is, properly speaking, evil, and there is no longer any possible redemption. Or rather redemption changes meaning: it is no longer the redemption of man and his sin, but that of the death of God. That death has to be atoned for (as in all cases where prophecy fails – Mühlmann[1]) by a compulsive effort of transformation of the world with a view to happiness. One must ensure one's salvation at all costs by realizing the world and by realizing oneself entirely (and here we come back to the problem of entire, integral reality). From this point on, Good and Evil, which were still opposing powers, but linked to each other in their straining towards transcendence, will be split, with a view to an optimal fulfilment, a definitive realization of the world under the sign of Good and Happiness. This has, in fact, merely a distant connection with the moral essence of Good, since Evil is driven out of it. Good of this kind no longer has anything moral about it, since it consists solely in the performance of happiness. The ideal of performance has taken over from moral self-surpassing – a new secular transcendence which completes that described by Max Weber in *The Protestant Ethic and the Spirit of Capitalism*, in which the world is transformed into value for the greater glory of God. In this case, the point is to make the world transparent and operational with no other aim than to root out all illusions and bad powers, all of Evil and the principle of Evil. In this way, under the hegemony of Good, everything is getting better and better and is, at the same time, going from bad to worse.

For this splitting of Good and Evil leads simultaneously, and in one and the same movement, to integral Good and integral Evil.

On the necessity of Evil and Hell

There is no longer any irrevocable damnation today. There is no longer any hell. We may concede that we are still within the mongrel concept of Purgatory, but virtually everything falls within the scope of redemption. It is clearly from such an evangelism that all the manifest, promotional signs of well-being and fulfilment derive that are offered us by a paradisaical society subject to the Eleventh Commandment ('Be happy and give all the signs of contentment!') – the one that cancels out all others. But we can also read this demand for salvation and universal atonement in the way that not only all current violence and injustices, but also, retrospectively, all the crimes and contradictory events of the past are now coming in for condemnation. The French Revolution is put in the dock and slavery is condemned, along with original sin and battered wives, the ozone layer and sexual harassment. In short, the pre-trial investigation for the Last Judgement is well under way. We are condemning, then pardoning and whitewashing, our entire history, exterminating the Evil from even the tiniest crevices in order to present the image of a radiant universe, ready to pass into the next world. A gigantic undertaking. One that is inhuman, superhuman, too human? As Stanislaw Lec says, 'We no doubt have too anthropomorphic a view of man.' And why feed this eternal repentance factory, this chain reaction of bad conscience? Because everything has to be saved. This is what we have come to today: everything will be redeemed, the entire past will be rehabilitated, polished to the point of transparency. As for the future, there's even better in store, and even worse: everything will be genetically modified to achieve biological perfection and the democratic perfection of the species. Salvation, which was defined by the equivalence of merit and grace, will, once the abscess of evil and hell has been drained, be defined by the equivalence between genes and performance.

Actually, once happiness becomes purely and simply the general equivalent of salvation, there is no further reason for heaven. No heaven without hell, no light without darkness. No one can be saved if no one is damned (by definition, but we also know this intuitively: where would the elect find pleasure, except in the contemplation of God, were it not for the spectacle of the damned and their torment?). And once everyone is virtually saved, no one is. Salvation no longer has any meaning. This is the fate in store for our democratic enterprise: it is vitiated from the outset by the neglect of necessary discrimination, by the omission of evil. We therefore need an irrevocable presence of Evil, an Evil with no possible redemption, a definitive discrimination, a perpetual duality of Heaven and Hell, and even in a way a predestination to Evil, for no destiny can be without some predestination. There is nothing immoral in this. By the rules of the game there is nothing immoral in some losing and others winning, nor even in everyone losing. What would be immoral would be for everyone to win. Now, this is the contemporary ideal of our democracy: that everyone be saved. And this is possible only at the cost of a perpetual upping of the stakes, of endless inflation and speculation, since ultimately happiness is not so much an ideal relationship to the world as a rivalry with, and a victorious relation to, others. And this is good: it means that the hegemony of Good, of the individual state of grace, will always be thwarted by some challenge or passion, and that any kind of happiness, any kind of ecstatic state, can be sacrificed to something more vital, which may be of the order of the will, as Schopenhauer has it, or of power, or of the will to power in Nietzsche's conception, but something which, in any event, is of the order of Evil, of which there is no definition, but which may be summed up as follows: that which, against any happy intended purpose [*destination heureuse*], is predestined to come to pass.

Beneath its euphoric exaltation, this imperative of optimum performance, of ideal achievement, certainly bears evil and misfortune within it, then, in the form of a profound disavowal of such fine prospects, in the form of a secret, anticipated disillusionment. Perhaps even this is again just a collective form of sacrifice – a human sacrifice, but a disembodied one, distilled into homeopathic doses.

Wherever humans are condemned to total freedom or to ideal fulfilment, this subversion seeps in – this automatic abreaction to their own good and their own happiness. When they are ordered to get the maximum efficiency and pleasure out of themselves, they remain out of sorts and live a split existence. In this strange world, where everything is potentially available (the body, sex, space, money, pleasure) to be taken or rejected *en bloc*, everything is there; nothing has disappeared physically, but everything has disappeared metaphysically. 'As if by magic or enchantment', you might say. Only the fact is, it is more by disenchantment. Individuals, such as they are, are becoming exactly what they are. With no transcendence and no image, they pursue their lives like a function that is useless in respect of another world, irrelevant even in their own eyes. And they do what they do all the better for the fact that there is no other possibility. No instance, no essence, no personal substance worthy of singular expression. They have sacrificed their lives to their functional existences. They coincide with the exact numerical calculation of their lives and their performances. An existence fulfilled, then, but one at the same time denied, thwarted, disavowed. The culmination of a whole negative counter-transference.

This imperative of optimum performance at the same time comes into internal contradiction with the democratic moral law which ordains that everyone be perpetually re-set to equality and everything re-set to zero, on the pretext of democracy and an equal sharing of opportunity and advantage. Given the prospect of salvation for all and universal redemption, no one has the right to distinguish himself, no one has the right to captivate [*séduire*]. For justice to be done, all privilege must disappear; it is for all to rid themselves voluntarily of any specific qualities, to become once again an elementary particle[2] – collective happiness, based on levelling down and repentance, leading to the coming of the lowest common denominator and basic banalities. This is like a

reverse potlatch, with everyone outdoing each other in mi
ism and victimhood, while fiercely cultivating their tiniest ͜
ences and cobbling together their multiple identities.

Repentance and recrimination are all part of the same movement: recrimination means going back over the crime to correct
its course and effects. This is what we are doing in going back
over the whole of our history, over the criminal history of the
human race, to do penance here and now as we await the Last
Judgement. For God is dead, but his judgement remains. Which
explains the immense syndrome of resipiscence and (historical)
rewriting (with the future genetic and biological rewriting of
the species still to come) that has seized the twentieth century's
end; with an eye, as ever, to deserving salvation and – with the
prospect of the final accounting before us – to presenting the
image of an ideal victim. Naturally, we are not speaking of a
real trial or of genuine repentance. It is a matter of fully enjoying
the spectacle of one's own misfortune: 'Mankind, which in
Homer's time was an object of contemplation for the Olympian
gods, now is one for itself. Its self-alienation has reached such a
degree that it can experience its own destruction as an aesthetic
pleasure of the first order' (Walter Benjamin).[3]

This is but the latest episode in a heart-rending process of
revisionism – running down not just the history of the twentieth
century, but all the violent events of past centuries, to subject
them to the new jurisdiction of human rights and crimes against
humanity (just as every action today is subjected to the jurisdiction of sexual, moral or political harassment). As part of the
same trend by which all works of art (including the human
genome) are listed as world heritage sites, everything is put on
the list of crimes against humanity.

The latest episode, then, of this revisionist madness has been the
proposal to condemn slavery and the slave trade as crimes against
humanity. An absurd proposal to rectify the past in terms of our
Western humanitarian consciousness or, in other words, in terms
of our own criteria, in the purest traditions of colonialism. This
imperialism of repentance really is the limit! The idea is, in
fact, to enable the 'peoples concerned' to put this tragedy behind

them thanks to this official condemnation and, once their rights have been restored and they have been recognized and celebrated as victims, to complete their work of mourning and draw a line under this page of their history in order to become full participants in the course of modernity. It might be seen, then, as a kind of successful psychoanalysis. Perhaps the Africans will even be able to translate this moral acknowledgement into damage claims, using the same monstrous measure of equivalence from which the survivors of the Shoah have been able to benefit. So we shall go on compensating, atoning and rehabilitating *ad infinitum*, and we shall merely have added to raw exploitation the hypocritical absolution of mourning; we shall merely, by compassion, have transformed evil into misfortune.

From the standpoint of our recycled humanism, the whole of history is pure crime – and, indeed, without all these crimes there quite simply would be no history: 'If we eliminated the evil in man,' wrote Montaigne, 'we would destroy the fundamental conditions of life.' But, on this basis, Cain killing Abel is already a crime against humanity – and almost a genocide (there were only two of them!), and isn't original sin already a crime against humanity? All this is absurd, all this humanitarian, retrospective fakery is absurd. And it all stems from the confusion between evil and misfortune. Evil is the world as it is and as it has been, and one may look upon this with lucidity. Misfortune is the world as it never should have been – but in the name of what? – in the name of what should be, in the name of God or a transcendent ideal, of a Good it would be difficult indeed to define. We may take a criminal view of crime – that is the tragic view – or we may take a recriminatory view – and that is the humanitarian view, the pathos-laden, sentimental view, the view which constantly calls for reparation. We have here all the *ressentiment* dredged up from the depths of a genealogy of morals, and requiring in us reparation for our own lives.

This retrospective compassion, this conversion of evil into misfortune is the twentieth century's most flourishing industry. First as a mental blackmailing operation, to which we all fall victim, even in our actions, from which we can now hope only for the lesser evil (keep a low profile, do everything in such a way as anyone else could have done it – decriminalize your existence!). Then as a profitable operation with gigantic yields, since misfortune (in all its forms: from suffering to insecurity, oppression to depression) represents a symbolic capital, the exploitation of which – even more than the exploitation of happiness – is endlessly profitable from the economic standpoint. It's a gold-mine, as they say, and there is an inexhaustible source of ore, because the seam lies within each of us. Misfortune commands the highest prices, whereas evil cannot be traded. It is impossible to exchange.

To transcribe evil into misfortune and then to transcribe misfortune into commercial, or spectacular, value – most often with the collusion or assent of the victim himself. But the victim's collusion with his own misfortune is part of the ironic essence of Evil. It is what brings it about that no one wants his own good, and nothing is for the best in the best of all worlds.

Notes

1 Untimely fragments

1 '. . . *comme on n'a qu'une seule idée dans sa vie*'. This comment is qualified subsequently.*

2 From his first book, *La Philosophie Tragique*, published in 1960 – he was just twenty – to his latest, *Loin de moi* (1999), Clément Rosset has constantly had, if we may put it this way, a single iron in the fire: that of an essentially joyful, unconditionally and totally life-affirming philosophy.

3 F. Nietzsche, *Beyond Good and Evil* (Harmondsworth: Penguin, 1990), p. 81.*

4 Pataphysics or, more properly, 'Pataphysics, was defined by Alfred Jarry as 'the science of imaginary solutions, which symbolically attributes the properties of objects, described by their virtuality, to their lineaments'.

5 Baudrillard attended the Lycée at Reims in the 1940s. Daumal, Gilbert-Lecomte and Vailland had been there in the 1920s, when they adopted the pseudonyms Nathaniel, Coco le Colchide and Dada respectively in 'le Grand Jeu', a made-up world of the imagination built around an invented character, Bubu, and also experimented with intoxicants. They founded a magazine entitled *Apollo*.*

6 The title is in fact *Une saison volée* and the novel was published by Gallimard in 1986.*

7 See *Ubu Cocu* (*Ubu Cuckolded*), esp. Act I, Scene IV.*

8 'I am not dealing with a museum piece from the history of philosophy. I believe the system has an application: it can serve as a means of thinking' (J. L. Borges, 'The Kabbalah', *Seven Nights*. Translated by Eliot Weinberger, with an introduction by Alistair Reid (London: Faber, 1986), p. 101).*

9 In Cyril Connolly and Simon Watson Taylor's translation, *Palotins* are rendered as 'Palcontents' and the *gidouille* as the 'strumpot'. See Alfred Jarry, *The Ubu Plays* (London: Eyre Methuen, 1968).*

2 'Activist' fragments

1 The BDIC at Nanterre holds a copy of a publication described as *Bulletin d'information* n° 2 (January 1964) issued by the 'Comité d'initiative pour une association populaire franco-chinoise'.*

2 The OAS (*Organisation de l'Armée Secrète*) was the pro-*Algérie française* grouping of right-wing extremists and dissident soldiers who waged a campaign of terror in France and Algeria in the 1960s.*

3 Lefebvre was attacked by the Situationists in *L'Internationale Situationniste* 10 (March 1966) for allegedly plagiarizing the 'Theses on the Paris Commune' published by Debord, Kotanyi and Vaneigem in March 1962.*

4 Selections from Baudrillard's writings for *Utopie* will be published by Verso in 2004.*

5 For Baudrillard's concept of the transpolitical, see his works *Fatal Strategies* (London: Pluto, 1990) and *The Transparency of Evil* (London: Verso, 1993).*

3 Aphoristic fragments

1 *Roland Barthes by Roland Barthes*. Translated by Richard Howard (Berkeley and Los Angeles: University of California Press, 1994), p. 94.*

2 The French here is *'la dérive urbaine'*. On this concept, see L. Andreotti (ed.), *Theory of the Dérive and other Situationist Writings on the City* (London: Atlantic Books, 1997).*

3 The articles by Raoul Vaneigem entitled 'Basic Banalities' parts I and II (*from Internationale Situationniste*, nos. 7 and 8 respectively) are translated in Ken Knabb (ed.), *Situationist International Anthology* (Berkeley: The Bureau of Public Secrets, 1981), pp. 89–100, pp. 118–33.*

4 From the Greek *akedia*, which means indifference or heedlessness, but also torpor or sluggishness. Transposed into Latin (*acedia*), then into French, the term will come to refer, in monastic parlance, to spiritual weariness.

5 J. Baudrillard, *America* (London: Verso, 1988).*

6 Baudrillard discusses Chuang-Tzu's (or, more properly, Zhuang-zi's) butcher in *Symbolic Exchange and Death* (London: Sage, 1993), pp. 119–21.*

7 In the original, Baudrillard speaks of the 'corpus glorieux', a play on the usual designation in religious discourse of the body of the risen Christ.*

8 Reprinted in J. Baudrillard, *Le ludique et le policier & autres écrits parus dans* Utopie *1967–1978* (Paris: Sens et Tonka, 2001), pp. 93–105.

9 'Die Rose ist ohne Warum./Sie blühet, weil sie blühet./Sie achtet nicht ihrer selbst,/fragt nicht, ob man sie siehet' (*Cherubinischer Wandersmann*, 1655, spelling modernized). This is my translation [CT].*

10 See F. Furet, *The French Revolution 1770–1814* (Oxford: Blackwell, 1996).*

11 The allusion here is, of course, to the debate in France about this book. For the English translation, see Stéphane Courtois et al., *The Black Book of Communism: Crimes, Terror, Repression* (Cambridge, Mass.: Harvard University Press, 1999).*

4 Fragments and fractals

1 J. Baudrillard, *Seduction*. Trans. Brian Singer (Basingstoke/London: Macmillan Education Ltd., 1990), p. 131.

2 Ibid., p. 132.

3 Ibid., p. 133.

4 The reference here is to fragment J273 from Lichtenberg's *Südelbücher*.*

5 See G. Bataille, *The Accursed Share* (3 vols.) (New York: Zone Books, 1988–93).*

6 See Macedonio Fernandez, *Papiers de Nouveauvenu et continuation du Rien* (Paris: José Corti, 1992). Very little of Fernandez's work is as yet translated into English, though there is one collection: *Selected Writings in Translation* (Fort Worth, Tex.: Latitudes, 1984).*

7 Baudrillard discusses Klossowski in 'Living Coin: Singularity of the Phantasm', in *Impossible Exchange* (London: Verso, 2001), pp. 121–31.*

8 See J. Baudrillard, 'When Bataille attacked the Metaphysical Principle of Economy', *Canadian Journal of Political and Social Theory* 11, 3 (1987), pp. 57–62.*

9 See Alexandre Kojève, *Introduction to the Reading of Hegel. Lectures on* The Phenomenology of Spirit. Assembled by Raymond Queneau. Edited by Allan Bloom. Translated by James H. Nichols Jnr. (Ithaca, NY and London: Cornell University Press, 1980).*

10 See Bataille, *Inner Experience* (Albany, NY: State University of New York Press, 1988).*

11 'Nationalization, the death penalty, denominational schools . . . outdated concerns of an old left that has long beavered away without success and has become covered, like a whale, with all the seaweed accumulated on its old journeys', *Le Monde*, 21 September 1983.

12 The reference is to fragment J 278 in the text established by Wolfgang Promies in his six-volume critical edition published by Hanser of Munich. This same reference system is adopted by Charles Le Blanc in the widely used French edition of the aphorisms: *Le Miroir de l'âme* (Paris: José Corti, 1997). I shall follow it here, even though the English translation cited, which includes fewer aphorisms, does not employ the same system.*

13 Fragment K 153. Cited in the translation by R. J. Hollingdale, *Georg Christoph Lichtenberg, Aphorisms* (Harmondsworth: Penguin, 1990), p. 174.*
14 This appears to be a reference to fragment L 402.*

5 Anthropological fragments

1 Baudrillard's debt to anthropology is examined in Gary Genosko, *Undisciplined Theory* (London: Sage, 1998), pp. 12–47.*
2 See *Cool Memories IV* (London: Verso, 2003), p. 42.*
3 Roland Barthes 'Inaugural Lecture' in Susan Sontag (ed.), *A Barthes Reader* (London: Vintage, 1982), pp. 461–2.
4 Jean Baudrillard, *In the Shadow of the Silent Majorities; or, The End of the Social and Other Essays*. Trans. Paul Foss, John Johnston and Paul Patton (New York: Semiotext(e), 1983).*
5 See Denis Hollier, *The College of Sociology (1937–1939)* (Minneapolis: University of Minnesota Press, 1988).
6 Bertrand Vergely, *La Souffrance* (Paris: Gallimard, 1997).
7 'A l'ombre du millénaire ou le suspense de l'an 2000', *D'un millénaire l'autre* (Paris: Albin Michel, 2000). An earlier version of this text appeared in translation in *Economy and Society*, 26, 4, November 1997: the relevant passage is on p. 448.*

6 Fateful fragments

1 J. Huizinga, *Homo Ludens. A study of the play element in culture* (London: Temple Smith, 1970), pp. 66–96.
2 J. Baudrillard, *Symbolic Exchange and Death* (London: Sage, 1993). See esp. pp. 177–80.
3 'Discussion sur le péché', *Dieu vivant*, no. 4, 1945. Republished in Georges Bataille, *Oeuvres complètes* VI (Paris: Gallimard, 1973). Marcel Moré, a 'nineteen-thirties non-conformist', who wrote on many subjects, held a kind of Salon on the quai de la Mégisserie in Paris. It was there, in his apartments in March 1944, that the 'Discussion on Sin' took place, a theologico-philosophical dispute revolving around Georges Bataille's fourteen fundamental theses on 'good and evil in their relation to being or beings', and the opposition to them on the part of the Jesuit, and future cardinal, Jean Daniélou. A rather lively discussion ensued between such different thinkers as Pierre Klossowski, Louis Massignon, Maurice de Gandillac, Arthur Adamov, Jean Hyppolite, Pierre Burgelin and Jean-Paul Sartre.

7 Fragments and viruses

1 This is a pastiche of José-Marie de Hérédia's famous lines: 'Propitious trade-winds bent their antennae/Towards the western world's mysterious rim' ('The Conquerors', *Cassell's Anthology of French Poetry*, selected and translated by Alan Conder, London, 1950).*

2 Baudrillard reviewed Marshall McLuhan's *Understanding Media* in 1967. A translation can be found in G. Genosko (ed.), *The Uncollected Baudrillard* (London: Sage, 2001), pp. 39–44.*

3 'ne fait pas événement'. This might have been rendered more colloquially as 'it has no impact', but I have generally tried to retain this reference to the event, which is a key notion for Baudrillard.*

4 *Cool Memories IV* (London: Verso, 2003), p. 24.

5 Ibid., p. 47.

6 See Charles Renouvier, *Uchronie, 1876* (Paris: Fayard, 1988).*

7 Nietzsche, *Beyond Good and Evil*. Trans. R. J. Hollingdale (Harmondsworth: Penguin, 1990), p. 162.*

8 Fragments of light

1 Walter Benjamin, 'A Small History of Photography', *One Way Street and Other Writings* (London: Verso, 1979), p. 250. The same passage appears in 'The Work of Art in the Age of Mechanical Reproduction' and is rendered as follows by Harry Zohn: 'If, while resting on a summer afternoon, you follow with your eyes a mountain range on the horizon or a branch which casts its shadow over you, you experience the aura of those mountains, of that branch' (*Illuminations*, pp. 224–5).*

2 Baudrillard's essay on 'The Art Conspiracy' can be found in *Screened Out* (London: Verso, 2002), pp. 181–5.*

3 Baudrillard has written on Warhol in 'Machinic Snobbery' in *The Perfect Crime* (London: Verso, 1996), pp. 75–85.*

4 The allusion here is to Duchamp's 'ready-mades', such as the famous *Fountain* of 1917, a factory-made urinal rotated through 90° and inscribed with the words 'R. Mutt 1917'. The argument is that Duchamp's break with art's previous frame of reference has been replicated generally in contemporary art practice.*

5 Baudrillard's writing on photography is now voluminous. A recent essay is 'Photography or Light-Writing: Literalness of the Image' in *Impossible Exchange* (London: Verso, 2001), pp. 139–47.*

6 Roland Barthes, *Camera Lucida. Reflections on Photography*. Trans. Richard Howard (London: Vintage, 1993), p. 95.*

7 The French term here is 'mise à plat', which can also mean a close-up or point-by-point examination.*

8 This is presumably a reference to that city's Festival of Photojournalism.*

9 *L'être-là.* The term of course came into French philosophical discourse from German [*Dasein*: existence].*

10 Henri Michaux (1899–1984), the Belgian-born French poet and artist whom Blanchot called 'l'ange du bizarre'.*

11 Walter Benjamin, 'A Small History of Photography', *One-Way Street.* Trans. Edmund Jephcott and Kingsley Shorter (London: Verso, 1997), p. 241.*

12 W. Benjamin, 'The Work of Art in the Age of Mechanical Reproduction', *Illuminations* (London: Fontana/Collins, 1973), p. 224. Since Baudrillard follows Benjamin's original French translator Pierre Klossowski and reads the term *Erscheinung* in the original German as 'appearance' rather than 'phenomenon', I have modified the translation accordingly. For the German original, see 'Das Kunstwerk im Zeitalter seiner technischen Reproduzierbarkeit [Dritte Fassung]', *Gesammelte Schriften*, vol. I–2, p. 479.*

13 Though the wording in the original French here differs somewhat from Klossowski's translation, this is presumably an allusion to the following passage: 'In dem Augenblick aber, da der Massstab der Echtheit an der Kunstproduktion versagt, hat sich auch die gesamte soziale Funktion der Kunst umgewälzt' ('Das Kunstwerk . . .', *Gesammelte Schriften*, I–2, p. 482).*

14 This is clearly a reference to Benjamin's discussion of Klee's 'Angelus Novus', with his face 'turned towards the past' in the ninth of his 'Theses on the Philosophy of History', *Illuminations* (London: Fontana/Collins, 1973), p. 259.*

15 Susan Sontag, *On Photography* (New York: Farrar, Straus & Giroux, 1977).

16 This seems to be a reference to Gaston Fernández Carrera, *La Photographie, Le Néant. Digressions autour d'une mort occidentale* (Paris: PUF, 1986).*

17 The term 'art photographique' seems to have entered the French language in May 1839 shortly after the English term 'photography' was coined (apparently by Sir John Herschel in March of that year).*

18 Paul Valéry, 'Le cimetière marin'. Quoted here in the version by Cecil Day-Lewis, 'The Graveyard by the Sea'.*

19 'Black bodies' are objects which do not reflect any light at any wavelength.*

9 Fragment fragments

1 The reference is presumably to Wilhlem E. Mühlmann, the German eth-
  nologist whom Baudrillard translated in the late 1960s. See Mühlmann,
  Messianismes révolutionnaires du tiers monde (Paris: Gallimard, 1968).*
2 *Les Particules élémentaires* was the French title of the Michel Houillebecq
  novel translated into English as *Atomised* (London: Vintage, 2001).*
3 'The Work of Art in the Age of Mechanical Reproduction', *Illuminations*,
  p. 244.*